AN SPSS COMPANION FOR *THE FUNDAMENTALS OF SOCIAL RESEARCH*

An SPSS Companion for The Fundamentals of Social Research offers students the opportunity to delve into the world of SPSS using real data sets and statistical analysis techniques directly from Paul M. Kellstedt, Guy D. Whitten, and Steven A. Tuch's new textbook. Workbook sections parallel chapters in the main text, giving students a chance to apply the lessons and techniques learned in each chapter in a statistical software setting. Detailed chapters teach students to reproduce results presented in the textbook, allowing them to become comfortable performing statistical analyses for evaluating causal claims through repeated practice. Step-by-step instructions for using SPSS are provided, along with command lines and screenshots to demonstrate proper use of the software. Instructions for producing the figures and tables in the main text are integrated throughout the workbook. End-of-chapter exercises encourage students to formulate and evaluate their own hypotheses.

Paul M. Kellstedt is a professor of political science at Texas A&M University.

Guy D. Whitten is a professor of political science and Director of the European Union Center at Texas A&M University.

Steven A. Tuch is a professor of sociology and public policy and public administration at George Washington University.

AN SPSS COMPANION FOR

The Fundamentals of Social Research

Paul M. Kellstedt

Texas A&M University

Guy D. Whitten

Texas A&M University

Steven A. Tuch

George Washington University

CAMBRIDGE
UNIVERSITY PRESS

University Printing House, Cambridge CB2 8BS, United Kingdom

One Liberty Plaza, 20th Floor, New York, NY 10006, USA

477 Williamstown Road, Port Melbourne, VIC 3207, Australia

314–321, 3rd Floor, Plot 3, Splendor Forum, Jasola District Centre,
New Delhi – 110025, India

103 Penang Road, #05–06/07, Visioncrest Commercial, Singapore 238467

Cambridge University Press is part of the University of Cambridge.

It furthers the University's mission by disseminating knowledge in the pursuit of
education, learning, and research at the highest international levels of excellence.

www.cambridge.org
Information on this title: www.cambridge.org/highereducation/isbn/9781009248204
DOI: 10.1017/9781009248181

© Paul M. Kellstedt, Guy D. Whitten, and Steven A. Tuch 2023

First published 2023

A catalogue record for this publication is available from the British Library.

ISBN 978-1-009-24820-4 Paperback

Brief Contents

Contents

Figures

Preface

This software companion book represents an effort to provide both extra exercises, as well as hands-on material for how to put the techniques that we discuss in *The Fundamentals of Social Research* into action. It is one of three workbooks, each written to help students to work with the materials covered in *The Fundamentals of Social Research* using a particular piece of statistical software.

This workbook focuses on using the program SPSS. (The other companion books are designed to work with Stata and R.) Our expectation is that the typical user of this book will be using a relatively recent version of SPSS on a computer that is running some version of the Windows operating system. We also have made an effort to accommodate users who are using some version of macOS or OS X. An online appendix available at www.cambridge.org/fsr will help Mac users with any difficulties.

The chapter structure of this workbook mirrors the chapter structure of *The Fundamentals of Social Research*. We have written with the expectation that students will read the chapters of this companion after they have read the chapters of the book.

We continue to update both the general and instructor-only sections of the webpage for our book (www.cambridge.org/fsr). As before, the general section contains data sets available in formats compatible with SPSS, Stata, and R. The instructor-only section contains several additional resources, including PowerPoint and TEX/Beamer slides for each chapter, a test bank, and answer keys for the exercises.

1 The Scientific Study of Society

1.1 OVERVIEW

In this chapter we introduce you to some of the important building blocks of a scientific approach to studying the social world. As you can already tell from reading the first chapter of *The Fundamentals of Social Research* – which we will refer to as "*FSR*" or the "main text" from here on – data are an important part of what we do both to explore the social world and to test hypotheses based on causal theories. An important part of working with data is learning how to use a statistical software package. In the sections that follow, we introduce you to the SPSS program and some basics that you will need to get up and running. In doing this, we also introduce some general principles of good computing practices for effectively working with data.

1.2 "A WORKBOOK? WHY IS THERE A WORKBOOK?"

You might be asking yourself this question, and it's perfectly fair to do so. Allow us to try to explain how this workbook fits in with the main *FSR* text.

As you will see in the weeks and months to follow in your class, the main textbook will teach you about the use of statistics in sociology and other social sciences, mostly by using equations and examples. So yes, in some ways, it will feel rather math-y. (And we think that's cool, though we realize that it's not everyone's cup of tea.) One of the ways that people learn about the practice of statistics is to use computer software to calculate statistics directly. To that end, many instructors want students to learn to use a particular computer software package so they can begin to conduct statistical analyses themselves.[1] We have discovered through years of teaching that this transition between equations in a book and software output on a computer screen is a very difficult one. The goal of this software companion book is to make this connection stronger, even seamless.

If we are successful, this book will do two things. First, it will teach the nuts and bolts about how to use SPSS. Though many (perhaps most) students today are quite computer-literate, we believe that having a reference guide for students to learn the techniques, or for them to teach themselves out of class time, will be helpful. Second, and more importantly, this software guide will provide explicit hand-holding to you as you learn to connect the key principles from the main text to the practical issues of producing and interpreting statistical results.

Each chapter of this software guide works in parallel with that of the main *FSR* text. So when you learn the equations of two-variable regression analysis in Chapter 10 of the main text, you will learn the details about using SPSS to estimate two-variable regression models in Chapter 10 of this companion book. And so on. In the end, we hope that the very important (but perhaps rather abstract) equations in the text become more meaningful to you as you learn to estimate the statistics yourself, and then to learn to interpret them meaningfully and clearly. Those three things – formulae, software, and interpretation – together provide a very solid foundation and basic understanding of social science.

Let's start.

1.3 GETTING STARTED WITH SPSS

To get started with SPSS, we recommend that you set yourself up in front of a computer that has the program installed with a copy of *FSR* close by. You should also have the set of computer files that accompany this text (which you can download from the text's website, www.cambridge.org/fsr) in a directory on the computer on which you are working. You will get the most out of this workbook by working in SPSS as you read this workbook.

The instructions in this book can help you learn SPSS whether you use a Windows-based PC or a Mac. Once the program is launched, SPSS works identically, no matter which platform you use. Windows-based PC users should be aware, though, that our screenshots will come from a Mac. Some of those screenshots that involve finding and opening files on your computer, therefore, will look somewhat unfamiliar to Windows users, but

---

[1] This particular software companion book teaches students to use SPSS, but we have also produced parallel books for instructors who wish to have their students learn Stata or R.

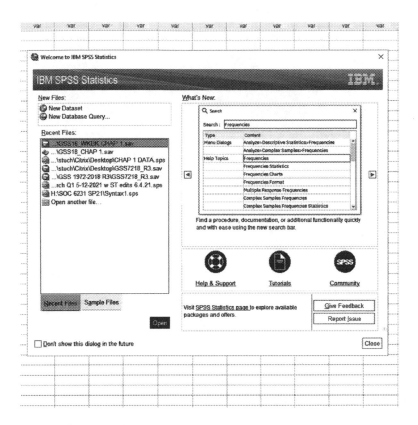

Figure 1.1 SPSS initial launch with recent files window

we assume that Windows users are at least somewhat used to this. Overall, the differences between running SPSS on Windows compared to a Mac are minimal.

Finally, we wrote this book while using version 28 of SPSS. Particularly for the statistical fundamentals you will learn in this book, the differences between versions – at least as old as SPSS 20 – are not severe. In fact, if you use any version of SPSS between 20 and 28, you might not notice the difference between what appears on your screen and what appears in the screenshots contained in this book.

1.3.1 Launching SPSS

When you are sitting in front of a computer on which SPSS has been properly installed, you can launch the program by double-clicking on the SPSS desktop icon (if one exists on your computer) or by finding the SPSS program on your Start menu, likely under "IBM SPSS Statistics." At this point, you should see one large window like that in Figure 1.1.

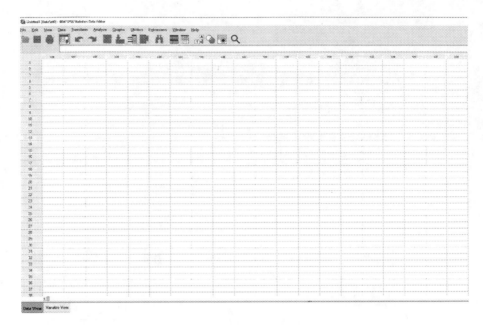

Figure 1.2 SPSS initial launch after closing recent files window

The large box in the middle of the screen enables you to open recent files that have been used on that computer. Since we assume that you're working in a lab or cluster computer, the simplest way to proceed is to simply close that window, either with the "Close" button in the lower-right corner or the "X" in the upper-right corner.

When you do that, you should see something very similar to what appears in Figure 1.2. It looks more or less like an empty spreadsheet, right? Some of the menu items (like "File" and "Edit") will look quite familiar, but others ("Transform," "Analyze," for example) will presumably be new to you. In addition, beneath the menu items, the row of icons will mostly appear unfamiliar – except, perhaps, the far-left icon that looks like an opening manilla folder. If you are seeing all of this, you are ready to go.

The part of the screen that looks like an empty spreadsheet is meaningful, especially the "empty" part. As you might guess, that's where the data that we will be analyzing will appear. As you also might guess, we haven't loaded any data into SPSS yet, hence the "empty." We'll get there soon enough.

1.3.2 Getting SPSS to Do Things by Using Pull-Down Menus

We will accomplish the vast majority of the tasks in SPSS by using the pull-down menus you see across the top of Figure 1.2. In our first foray into the program, we are simply going to open a data set. This means that we need to start by clicking on the textual heading "File," then "Open," and then "Data." In Figure 1.3, we show what this will look like.

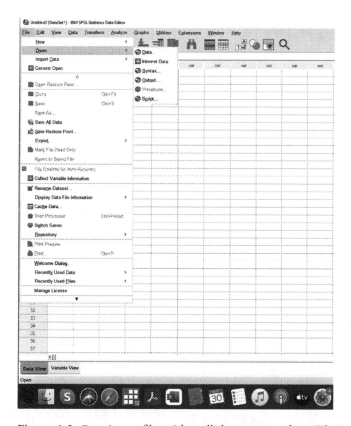

Figure 1.3 Opening a file with pull-down menu for "File," "Open," and "Data" selected

Alternatively, you can just click on the icon that looks like a folder being opened, right below "File." Either way, you'll see a pop-up box open up that looks like what we see in Figure 1.4. Throughout this workbook, on the computer on which this workbook was created, these files are located in the folder "FSRSPSSFiles."

The initial data set that we wish to open is named "African American Home Ownership 1985-2014.sav," so once we see that file, as you can in Figure 1.4, we click on "African American Home Ownership 1985-2014.sav" and then click the "Open" button. The ".sav" portion of the file name denotes that the file is in the format of an SPSS data set.[2]

You may have noticed that, when you opened the data set, SPSS launched an additional window. This is an important part of how SPSS works. When you execute a command in SPSS, it appears in what we will call the "output window." You can toggle back and forth between the main window and the output window by hovering over the SPSS icon in

---

[2] Like most software programs, SPSS can import data sets that are created with other types of software. To do that, you would click "File," "Import data," and then choose the format that you're trying to import and follow along as pop-up boxes open. If you want to continue to use imported files in SPSS, you might wish, once a file is imported, to "Save As" an SPSS .sav file. ("Save as" is also under the "File" menu.)

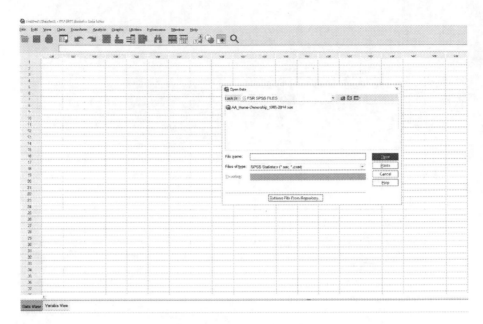

Figure 1.4 Pop-up menu for opening a file in SPSS

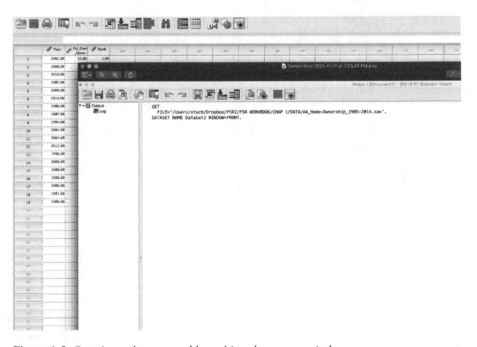

Figure 1.5 Opening a data set and launching the output window

your task tray in Windows. Figure 1.5 shows the main window of SPSS with the output window layered on top of it. Every command you run in SPSS will generate some type of output, and all of that output will be shown in that output window. You will be able to edit the output – we'll

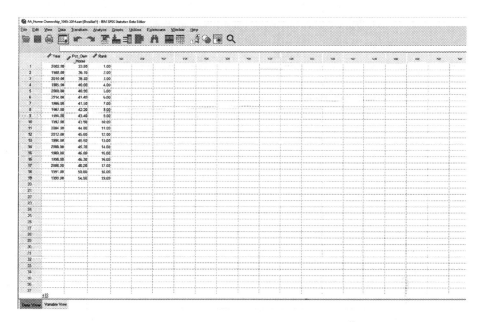

Figure 1.6 Main window view of the "African American Home Ownership 1985–2014.sav" data set

show you how to do that eventually. This happens frequently, actually, even with experienced data analysts, because we often run some type of data analysis and then realize we wished we had done something else. Saving or printing the results of the output window is also easy, and we'll show you how to do that, too.

For the moment, let's simply minimize the output window by just clicking on the "_" (minimize) portion of the output window near the top right. That will leave us with the main SPSS window where we will eventually do our analysis. That view is displayed in Figure 1.6.

1.3.3 Initially Examining Data in SPSS

Now that we have shown you how to get data into SPSS, we want you to take a look at the data that you have loaded into the program.[3] These data are from the 1985–2014 General Social Surveys (GSS), a data set that you will become quite familiar with in your statistics course because we make extensive use of it in this workbook as well as in the main text. The particular survey question that we examine in this illustration asks respondents whether they own or rent the dwelling in which they currently live.

---

[3] We discuss how to manually enter your own data into an SPSS file in an online appendix, available at www.cambridge.org/fsr.

In Figure 1.6, you will see data in three columns, labeled from left to right as "Year," "Pct_Own_Home," and "Rank." Those labels correspond to the names of the three variables in our data set. Down the rows you will see the cases of the three variables. For example, in row 10 of the data window, which is the tenth case in the data set, we see the following values for the three variables. "Year" takes on the value of 1993, "Pct_Own_Home" has the value of 43.90, and "Rank" has the value 10.00. These variable names make clear what each variable represents and what the corresponding values mean.

You can use the bars at the right and at the bottom of the data set to scroll through it. As you already know, this data set has only three variables, so you don't need to scroll to the right to see any other variables. However, you can use the bar at the right of the screen to scroll down when you have larger data sets. For now, you'll notice that the last of our cases has a value for "Year" of 1990 and a value for "Pct_Own_Home" of 54.90. You can also see that the data set has a total of nineteen cases.

In the lower-left portion of Figure 1.6, you will notice that there are two tabs – on the left, in a dark gray color, is "Data View" (the view that is currently active, as you might guess, because you're viewing the data), and on the right, in light gray, is "Variable View." Click on the "Variable View" tab. You will notice a few things, including that the colors have reversed themselves, with the "Data View" now in light gray, and the "Variable View" in dark gray. More importantly, we are no longer looking at the columns of data, but instead at the description of the variables in the data set. It should look like Figure 1.7.

Several things are worth mentioning. First, the variable names that were formerly across the top in columns under the "Data View" are now down the left in rows in "Variable View." And there are details about what each of those variables mean. In particular, notice the "Label," "Values," and "Missing" columns. The "Label," as you might guess, is the label of the variable. In our data set, none of the variables have labels because they are all self-explanatory. Also, under "Values," and "Missing," you will note that all of the cells say "None." The "Values" option will be useful later on, and we will refer to it frequently in this companion. There are no labels for the values here, because, for all three variables, the values speak for themselves. If, for any of the cases, we could not obtain data for any reason for the values of a variable, we would need a category for that to let SPSS know that the value is missing. Typically, researches use a value like "98" or "99" to denote a missing case. If any of our variables had missing cases, and the "Missing" cell for that variable read "98," then SPSS would know to conduct whatever analysis using that variable without making reference to that particular case. Again, these features will come into play in subsequent chapters with other data sets.

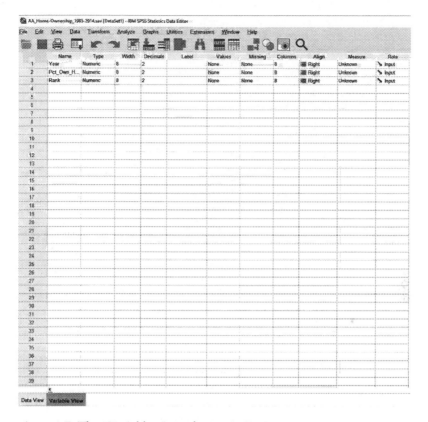

Figure 1.7 The "Variable View" feature in SPSS

1.3.4 Saving Output and Exiting the Program

To save the results of our output window, from Figure 1.5, we can just click on the icon that looks like an old-style floppy disk, or click on "File," followed by "Save." One thing to note is that SPSS will not default to saving your output in the same place where the data are stored, so use the pull-down menu as above to find the correct drive and directory where you want your output saved. Your screen should look similar to Figure 1.8.

Another caution: SPSS defaults to saving its output as an "SPSS Viewer File," which means you can only see it on a computer that has an SPSS license on it. So if you were to save your output from a lab onto a memory stick or a folder in the Cloud, you would only be able to view the output if you were on another computer with an SPSS license. As a result, we recommend using the pull-down menu next to the "Save as type" option, and saving files as .html files (what SPSS will call an "SPSS Web Report"). That detail is displayed in Figure 1.9.

You can exit SPSS by clicking the "X" in the top right of the program, and it will prompt you to see if you're sure you want to exit, and if any file changes need to be saved.

You are now ready to proceed to the end-of-chapter exercises.

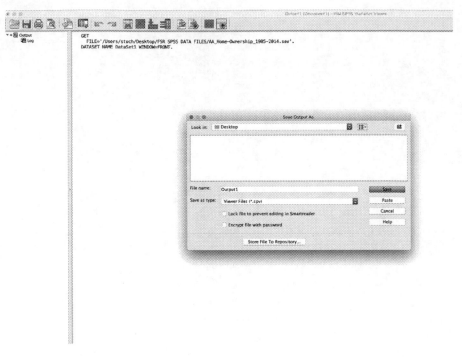

Figure 1.8 How to save your output in SPSS

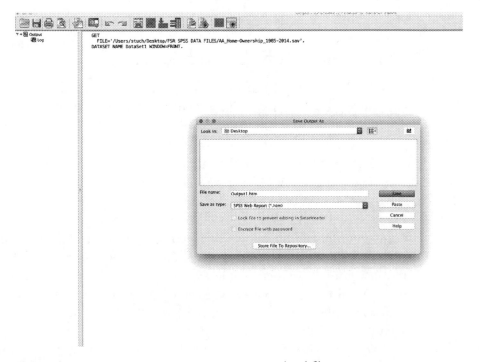

Figure 1.9 How to save your output in SPSS as an .html file

1.4 EXERCISES

1. Go through all of the steps described above. Once you have the "Data View" open (so that your computer looks like Figure 1.6), do the following:

(a) Look at the values in the column labeled "Pct_Own_Home." This is our measure of homeownership. Do the following:

   i. Identify the year with the highest value for this variable.

   ii. Identify the year with the lowest value for this variable.

   iii. What does it mean if this variable goes up by one?

(b) Look at the values in the column labeled "Rank." This is our measure of the rank, from lowest to highest, of the proportion of African American homeownership in the years from 1985 to 2014. Now do the following:

   i. Identify the year with the highest value for this variable.

   ii. Identify the year with the lowest value for this variable.

   iii. What does it mean if this variable goes up by one?

2 The Art of Theory Building

2.1 OVERVIEW

One of our emphases in *FSR* has been on producing new causal theories, and then evaluating whether or not those theories are supported by evidence. In this chapter, we describe how to explore sources of variation – both across space, and across time – to get you started thinking about new explanations for interesting phenomena. We also help you explore how new theories can be built upon the existing work in the literature.

2.2 EXAMINING VARIATION ACROSS TIME AND ACROSS SPACE

As we discuss in Section 2.3 of *FSR*, one way to develop ideas about causal theories is to identify interesting variation. In that section, we discuss examining two types of variation, cross-sectional and time-series variation. In this section, we show you how to create figures like the ones presented in Section 2.3 of *FSR*. Although there are many different types of graphs that can be used to examine variation in variables, we recommend a bar graph for cross-sectional variation and a connected plot for time-series variation.

2.2.1 Producing a Bar Graph for Examining Cross-Sectional Variation

A useful way to get a sense of the variation for a cross-sectional variable is to produce a bar graph in which you display the values of that variable across spatial units. In the example that we display in Figure 2.2 of *FSR*, we have a bar graph of Gini coefficients in 2013 for twenty-three randomly selected nations. Building on what we learned in Chapter 1, we will now show you how to produce a figure like this in SPSS. The first step to doing this is opening the data.

As was the case in Chapter 1, all of the data files that we will use are located in the directory "FSRSPSSFiles" on the computer that created this

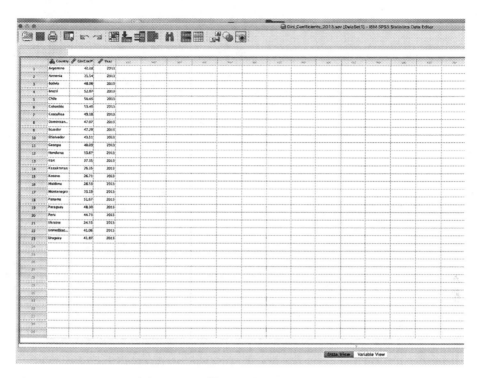

Figure 2.1 First view of the Gini coefficients data set

workbook. We encourage you to follow this practice for the sake of convenience. To navigate to that folder, we use the pull-down menus – "File" then "Open" then "Data" – as described in Chapter 1, and then change the drive and directory as necessary until we find the correct location where the data set is stored. The data file is called "Gini_coefficients_2013.sav." Once you've found it, open it.

Your screen should look like Figure 2.1. So let's build a graph like the one in Figure 2.2 of *FSR*.[1] We build a graph in SPSS using the "Graph" command at the top of the toolbar. So click on "Graph," and, in the pull-down menu, click on "Chart Builder...." At this point, a dialog box might open cautioning you to be careful about measurement levels of your variables. If so, click "OK" to proceed.

The "Chart Builder" dialog box will appear, as in Figure 2.2 here. As you can see from Figure 2.2 in *FSR*, we want to build a bar chart here. In

---

[1] You might notice that the graph we produce here will not look exactly like the one in the main textbook, and that's okay in this case. That figure was generated using a different software program, so we will be doing our best to approximate that figure. This issue will crop up repeatedly throughout this workbook, and we encourage you to not worry about it. In fact, what you'll almost universally notice is that the output is remarkably similar – just not identical.

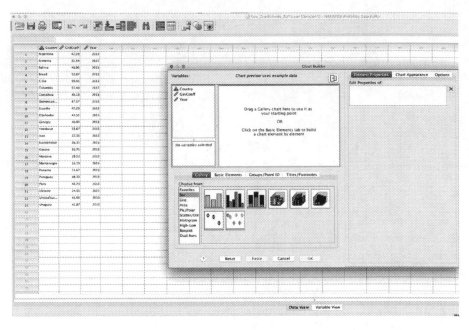

Figure 2.2 SPSS's Chart Builder

SPSS's Chart Builder, we choose the type of chart – Bar, Line, Histogram, etc. – from the lower-left pane of the dialog box. The "Bar" option should be the default choice. (If something else happens to be selected on your screen, though, click on "Bar" on the lower-left under the "Gallery" tab.) The next tab to the right is the "Basic Elements" tab, where we define what we want our bar graph to look like. Click on "Basic Elements." When you do that, you'll see two sub-tabs, one in which we will "Choose Axes," and the other in which we will "Choose Elements."

As you will see, there are several options for each category, and they are displayed here in Figure 2.3. Under "Choose Axes," we want a simple two-dimensional $X–Y$ chart, so double-click on the top-right of those five choices (as seen in Figure 2.3). Under "Choosing Elements," we want bars, so double-click the option that looks like vertical bars. Please note that it's essential to double-click both of these options, not merely click on them once.

Double-clicking both of those decisions of "Basic Elements" will produce a screen that looks like that in Figure 2.4. You'll see a rudimentary bar chart in the top-left pane of the dialog box. But we haven't yet told SPSS what variables we want in the chart. Let's do that now.

As you can see from Figure 2.2 of *FSR*, the X-axis variable is the country, and the Y-axis variable is the Gini coefficient. We define those variables in the chart by grabbing them with our mouse from the list

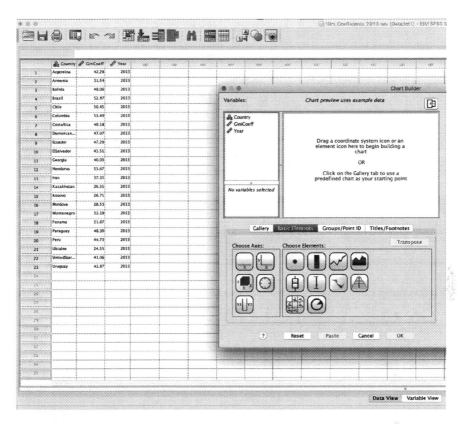

Figure 2.3 The "Basic Elements" tab of SPSS's Chart Builder

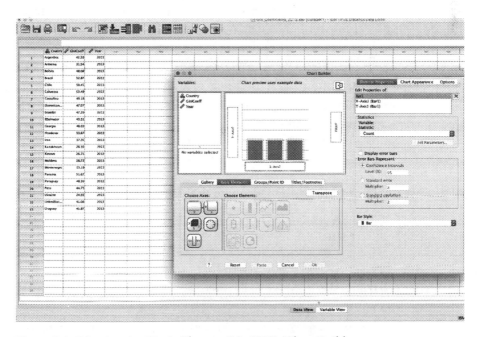

Figure 2.4 Selecting the "Basic Elements" in SPSS's Chart Builder

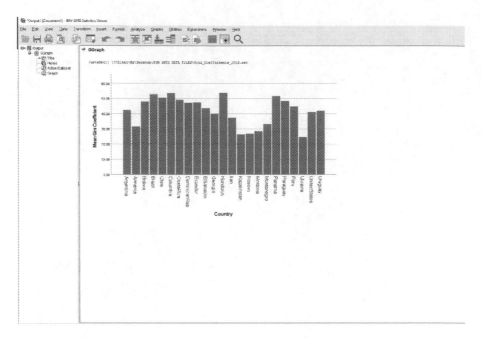

Figure 2.5 Initial graph of Gini coefficients in SPSS's Chart Builder

of variables in the top left of the dialog box and dragging them to the appropriate (*X* or *Y*) axis and dropping them there. So go ahead and do that. Grab the variable labeled "GiniCoeff [GiniCoeff]" and drag and drop it onto the *Y* (vertical) axis. Next, grab the variable labeled "country" and drag and drop it onto the *X* (horizontal) axis.

Now let's see what this looks like, just as a first cut, and note how it compares to Figure 2.2 in *FSR*. Click on the "OK" button at the bottom of the dialog box and let's find out. You will notice that the output window appeared, and a command sequence appears, and the graph (though you might have to scroll down to see it). Sometimes it helps to maximize the output window to get a fuller view, as we have done in Figure 2.5.

In the output window, if you left-click your mouse one time inside the graph, it selects the entire graph. Then, if you right-click your mouse once, you'll be able to copy it to your computer's clipboard, and paste it elsewhere (like a word processor) if you need to. Alternatively, if you right-click, you will also see the option to "Export. . ." the graph. You can export the file to a Word document, an Excel spreadsheet, an Adobe .pdf file, or (if you select the "None (Graphics only)" option) you can export the graph as a high-resolution graphics image such as a .png, .tif, .bmp, or .jpg file (among other types).

When displaying data in graphs, it is important that you do so in a fashion that allows you and your readers to most easily make the

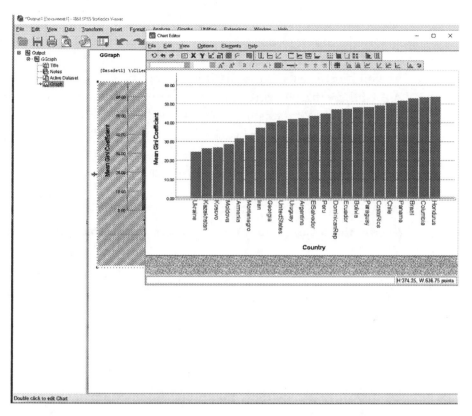

Figure 2.6 Launching SPSS's Chart Editor. (Well spotted if you notice that there are some slight differences from Figure 2.2 in *FSR*: the country names there face the other way and some minor corrections have been made.)

assessments that you and they want to make. In this case, we want to see what makes the citizens of a country be more or less economically equal. Try comparing the value of the Gini coefficient between Peru and Ecuador in the graph that we just made, Figure 2.5. Not an easy thing to do! It's a lot easier using Figure 2.2 from *FSR* because the cases have been *sorted*.

Fortunately, SPSS allows us to sort the bars to our liking. For example, let's say that, instead of arranging nations alphabetically, as we did in Figure 2.2 in *FSR* and in Figure 2.5 here, you prefer to display the countries along a continuum from the smallest to the largest Gini coefficients instead. To do so, from the output window where we see our bar chart, double-click the chart, which will launch "Chart Editor" mode. That appears in Figure 2.6. Because we want to change the X axis, we click on the blue "X" in the toolbar to "Select the X axis." From there, select the "Categories" tab; then, under "Sort by," use the pull-down menu to select "Statistic"; then click "Apply" and then "Close." You will notice that, when we click the "X" in the top-right corner to close our Chart Editor, our edited chart now appears in our SPSS output. From here, you can also save or export the graph in the same way as mentioned above. The choice as to which graph to use is ours. In this case, in order to make comparisons of Gini coefficients across nations easier – try comparing the value of the Gini coefficients between Montenegro and Armenia in the graph in Figure 2.2 in *FSR* – we might opt for the display in Figure 2.6 here.

At this point, we're reasonably close to exactly reproducing Figure 2.2 from *FSR*. You will notice a few small differences, though, and you could experiment with the Chart Editor to rectify those differences should you care to do so.

2.2.2   Producing a Connected Plot for Examining Time-Series Variation

A useful way to get a sense of the variation for a time-series variable is to produce a connected plot in which you display the values of that variable *connected* across time. In the example that we display in Figure 2.1 of *FSR*, we have a connected plot of the values for U.S. presidential approval each month from February 1995 to December 2005. Building on what we learned in Chapter 1, we will now show you how to produce a figure like this in SPSS. As with the previous example, the first step to doing this is to load the data into SPSS.

Because we already have data from the previous example in active memory, we first have to tell SPSS that we want to use a different dataset. We do that by using the "File" menu, then "New" and "Data," and the previous example's data are removed.

Again, the data are located in the directory "C:\FSRSPSSFiles" on the computer that created this workbook. To navigate to that folder, we use the pull-down menus – "File" then "Open" then "Data" – and then change the drive and directory as necessary until we find the correct location where the data set is stored. The data file is called "presap9505.sav." Once you've found it, open it.

As before, we'll build a graph in SPSS using the "Graph" command at the top of the toolbar. So click on "Graph," and in the pull-down menu, click on "Chart Builder...." Again, if a dialog box opens cautioning you to be careful about measurement levels of your variables, click "OK" to proceed. The "Chart Builder" dialog box will appear.

As you can see from Figure 2.1 in *FSR*, we want to build a line chart here. So, in Chart Builder, we choose the type of chart – in this case "Line" – from the lower-left pane of the dialog box. In the "Line" box, there are two types. Double-click the one on the left – "Simple Line" – and SPSS will begin to build the chart.

Your screen should look like that in Figure 2.7. Next, in the top pane of the Chart Builder, let's define the axes. Grab, drag, and drop the "presap"

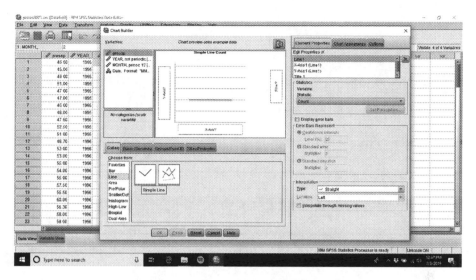

Figure 2.7 Beginning to build a line graph using SPSS's Chart Builder

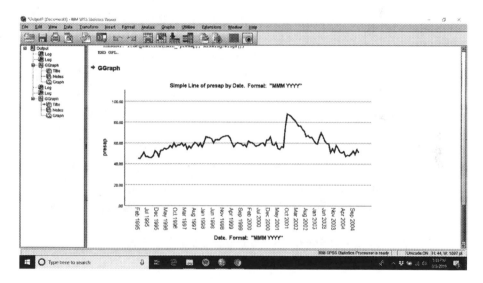

Figure 2.8 A first cut at a line graph of presidential approval

variable from the variable list onto the Y (vertical) axis, and then grab, drag, and drop the "Date" variable onto the X (horizontal) axis. Click "OK" and let's see what we've got as a first cut.

Our output screen is presented in Figure 2.8. Tastes for how a graph should appear can (to some extent) vary, but a few items of this first effort leave us wanting to do better. In particular, the title of the chart (that was inserted by default) is a bit cumbersome. (We prefer to leave our charts without titles, and then insert a caption with the figure, as we have in both

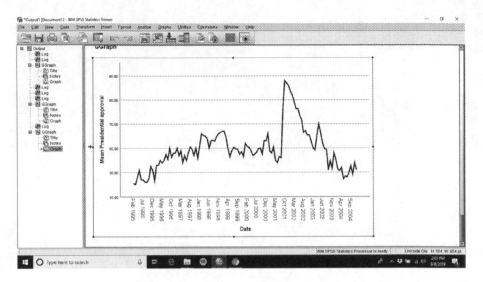

Figure 2.9 A better (to us) line graph of presidential approval

this companion book and the main *FSR* text.) Also, in our view, the range on the *Y* axis – from 0 to 100 – seems like a waste of visual space to us.[2]

We can edit the chart as we did in the previous section by double-clicking the chart and entering the Chart Editor. Removing the title is as simple as left-clicking on it one time, then hitting the Delete key on your keyboard. We can edit the *Y* axis by hitting the blue "Y" in the toolbar, which will open up a "Properties" dialog box. Click on the "Scale" tab, and in the "Minimum" box, type 40, and in the "Maximum" box, type 90. Click "Apply," and then "Close," and you have (in our eyes) a much better-looking chart. It should look like our screen in Figure 2.9.

At this point, we're reasonably close to exactly reproducing Figure 2.1 from *FSR* (see footnote 1 on page 13). As before, you can also save or export the graph in the same way as mentioned above.

2.3 USING GOOGLE SCHOLAR TO SEARCH THE LITERATURE EFFECTIVELY

We assume that you're skilled at web searches, likely using Google's search engine. In addition to the myriad other things that Google allows us to search for on the Internet, it has a dedicated search engine for scholarly publications like books and journal articles. The aspects of Google you're likely most familiar with come from Google's home page, www.google .com. The searches that they enable through scholarly work, however,

---

[2] Others might like the 0–100 range, because it represents the true theoretical range of the variable's minimum and maximum. To each their own.

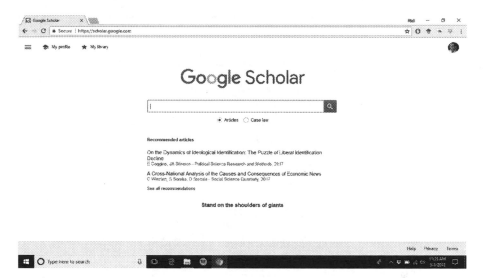

Figure 2.10 The Google Scholar home page

using what they call "Google Scholar," is at a different site, https://
scholar.google.com. That site looks a good bit like Google's home page,
but when you're at Google Scholar, it's searching a different corner of
the Internet entirely – the part where academic journals and books are
uploaded.

Figure 2.10 shows the Google Scholar home page. If you have a Google
account (like a gmail address), you can save items in "My Library" – we'll
show you how to do that shortly – that you can access any time. The articles
are normally saved as an Adobe .PDF file. You'll notice the familiar search
box that looks like Google's normal home page. You can tell from the
figure, though, that, despite the similarities in appearances, this website is
https://scholar.google.com.

So let's see how Google Scholar works. In the first chapter of *FSR*,
we introduced you to what we called the theory of economic threat
and attitudes toward immigrants. Let's see what happens when we type
"economic threat and attitudes toward immigrants" in the Google Scholar
search bar.

Figure 2.11 shows the results of that Google Scholar search. Let's
examine that result. If you look to the far right of the fifth selection (the
article by Bobo and Fox), you see the text "[PDF] jstor.org," which shows
you what format the file is available in – in this case, an Adobe .PDF –
and where – in this case, at the archive www.jstor.org. Your college or
university's library almost surely has a subscription to JStor that your
student fees pay for, and so, if you're on a campus Internet connection
(as opposed to a WiFi network at your home, or on a cellular network),
clicking on "[PDF] jstor.org" will take you to the article. (If you're on

Figure 2.11 Google Scholar results for "economic threat and attitudes toward immigrants" search

your home WiFi network, then JStor doesn't know that you're a university student, and the publisher might ask you to pay a rather steep fee for access to the article. So beware about where you can do these searches for free.)

There's a lot of other information that the Google Scholar search reveals, though. First, if you want to save an entry to your "My Library," then click on the ☆ at the lower left of the item, and you'll be able to access that .PDF anywhere.

Importantly, you can also see how influential every article has been to date. In Figure 2.11, you can see text near the bottom of the first citation (the article by Esses et al.) that says "Cited by 1117" – which means that the article has been cited 1117 times to date.[3] That number indicates that the paper has been massively influential.[4]

---

[3] If you conduct that same search today, the number would surely be higher. Citations tend to accumulate over time.

[4] Of course, you should be careful to remember the original publication date when interpreting citation counts as a measure of impact. The Esses et al. article was published

Of course, that doesn't necessarily mean that the 1117 other articles all cite the Esses et al. (2001) article approvingly. Some might; others might not. But being agreed with, or being "proved right," isn't the highest value in science. It's far better to be an influential part of an ongoing debate while being proved wrong in some respects, than it is to be indisputably correct but ignored by other scholars.

Perhaps you say to yourself, "Sure, Esses and her colleagues wrote an influential article on economic threat and attitudes toward immigrants a good long while ago. What kind of work is being done on the topic *now*?" This is one of the places where Google Scholar is fabulous. That "Cited by 1117" is clickable. You can literally see the list of all 1117 articles that cite the Esses article if you want. (Of course, it would take you a while to sift through them!) If you click on "Cited by 1117" and then choose "Since 2017" on the left side of the screen, you will see the number of citations that the Esses article has received since 2017. (You can pick "since" any year you like, obviously.) This is a good way to start the process of exploring a particular topic in academic writing that interests you.

Just like with using any Internet search engine, there's something of a skill in figuring out how to efficiently search for the material you want without getting bogged down with lots of results that aren't interesting to you. Should you use quotation marks in your search, or in a portion of your search terms? Sometimes yes, sometimes no. (In the example above, we did not.) As a general rule, it might be best to try it both ways to see if you get different results.

We have not exhausted all there is to know about how to use Google Scholar here, of course. For example, many scholars have created "Google Scholar profiles," which enables you to see the list of scholarly articles and books that they have authored, usually sorted from those with the most citations to the ones with the least. This can help you find similar articles, too, because many scholars work on a topic over the course of many years, and therefore their earlier articles are related to their more recent ones. In Figure 2.11, for example, you can see the scholars whose names are underlined; those are clickable links to those scholars' respective Google Scholar profiles. In addition, the "Help" section of Google Scholar is surprisingly helpful!

---

in 2001, so it's not as if some scholars who work in this area have somehow not yet heard of this article. But for an article published more recently – say in 2016 – its impact cannot yet fully be known. That merely means that we don't yet know if the article is likely to have a large impact. Only time will tell.

2.4 WRAPPING UP

In the main *FSR* text, we discussed how important it is that our theories be new and original – that is, that we aren't merely repeating the ideas and claims of previous scholars. One of the important preconditions for doing something genuinely new is to be familiar with the works that have already been produced on that same topic. Having the vast archive of journal articles and even many books available online – and freely accessible, thanks to your university's libraries – through storage sites like www.jstor .org has been the first step in making this task a lot easier than it was in decades past. The second step has been the invention of very sophisticated search engines like Google Scholar to help us find the previous studies that we otherwise might have missed.

2.5 EXERCISES

1. Conduct a search for the following terms using both Google's home page (www.google.com) and Google Scholar (https://scholar.google.com). Only include the quotation marks in your search if we include them. Report the similarities and differences you observe in the first page of the search results:

   (a) "economic threat and attitudes toward immigrants"

   (b) economic threat and attitudes toward immigrants

   (c) economic threat and prejudice

2. Launch SPSS and open the "Gini_Coefficients_2013.sav" data set.

   (a) Once you have done this, follow the steps above to reproduce – as nearly as possible – the graph presented in Figure 2.2 from *FSR*. Open a word processing document and then copy the figure from SPSS and paste it into your word processing document.

   (b) Write a short summary of what you see in this figure.

3. Launch SPSS and open the "presap9505.sav" data set.

   (a) Once you have done this, follow the steps above to reproduce – as nearly as possible – the graph presented in Figure 2.1 from *FSR*. Open a word processing document and then copy the figure from SPSS and paste it into your word processing document.

   (b) Write a short summary of what you see in this figure.

3 Evaluating Causal Relationships

OVERVIEW

Unlike the previous two chapters, in Chapters 3 through 6, there will not be any computer-based lessons in SPSS. Not to worry, though. There will be more than enough time for intensive computer work later in the book. We promise!

In this abbreviated chapter, then, we offer some expanded exercises that will apply the lessons learned in the main text, and build on the skills from the first two chapters.

3.2 **EXERCISES**

1. Causal claims are common in media stories about news and politics. Sometimes they are explicitly stated, but often they are implicit. For each of the following news stories, identify the key causal claim in the story, and whether, based on the information given, you are convinced that all four causal hurdles have been crossed. (But remember that most media stories aren't the original generators of causal claims; they merely report on the news as they see fit to do so.)

    (a) www.cnn.com/2018/01/16/politics/freedom-house-democracy-trump-report/index.html

    (b) https://thehill.com/opinion/energy-environment/368355-wheres-the-proof-climate-change-causes-the-polar-vortex

    (c) www.foxnews.com/us/2018/01/16/california-mudslides-where-and-why-happen.html

    (d) www.aljazeera.com/news/2018/01/trump-muslim-ban-shifted-public-opinion-study-finds-180113092728118.html

    (e) www.npr.org/player/embed/575959966/576606076 (Podcast)

2. Candidates for public office make causal claims all the time. For each of the following snippets from a key speech made by a candidate, identify the key causal claim made in the speech, and whether, based on the information given, you are convinced that all four causal hurdles have been crossed. (But remember that candidates for office are not scientists responsible for testing causal claims; they are trying to persuade voters to support them over their opponent.)

    (a) "America is one of the highest-taxed nations in the world. Reducing taxes will cause new companies and new jobs to come roaring back into our country. Then we are going to deal with the issue of regulation, one of the greatest job-killers of them all. Excessive regulation is costing our country as much as $2 trillion a year, and we will end it. We are going to lift the restrictions on the production of American energy. This will produce more than $20 trillion in job creating economic activity over the next four decades." (Excerpt from Donald Trump's speech accepting the Republican nomination for President, July 21, 2016.)

    (b) "Now, I don't think President Obama and Vice President Biden get the credit they deserve for saving us from the worst economic crisis of our lifetimes. Our economy is so much stronger than when they took office. Nearly 15 million new private-sector jobs. Twenty million more Americans with health insurance. And an auto industry that just had its best year ever. That's real progress." (Excerpt from Hillary Clinton's speech accepting the Democratic nomination for President, July 28, 2016.)

    (c) "The truth is, on issue after issue that would make a difference in your lives – on health care and education and the economy – Sen. McCain has been anything but independent. He said that our economy has made 'great progress' under this president. He said that the fundamentals of the economy are strong. And when one of his chief advisers – the man who wrote his economic plan – was talking about the anxiety Americans are feeling, he said that we were just suffering from a 'mental recession,' and that we've become, and I quote, 'a nation of whiners.'" (Excerpt from Barack Obama's speech accepting the Democratic nomination for President, August 28, 2008.)

    (d) "His [Barack Obama's] policies have not helped create jobs, they have depressed them. And this I can tell you about where President Obama would take America: His plan to raise taxes on small business won't add jobs, it will eliminate them; … And his trillion-dollar deficits will slow our economy, restrain employment, and cause wages to stall." (Excerpt from Mitt Romney's speech accepting the Republican nomination for President, August 30, 2012.)

3. Social science, as we have argued, revolves around the making and evaluation of causal claims. Find each of the following research articles – Google Scholar

makes it easy to do so – and then identify the key causal claim made in the article. Then produce a causal hurdles scorecard, and decide to what degree you are convinced that all four causal hurdles have been crossed. Some of the statistical material presented in the articles will, this early in the semester, be beyond your comprehension. That will change as the semester rolls along! (And remember that social scientists are trained to be experts in testing causal claims. So set the bar high.)

(a) Scarborough, W.J., Pepin, J.R., Lambouths III, D.L., Kwon, R., and Monasterio, R. 2021. "The intersection of racial and gender attitudes, 1977 through 2018." *American Sociological Review* 86(5):823–855.

(b) Perry, S.L., Cobb, R.J., Whitehead, A.L., and Grubbs, J.B. 2021 "Divided by faith (in Christian America): Christian nationalism, race, and divergent perceptions of racial injustice." *Social Forces*, soab134, https://doi.org/10.1093/sf/soab134.

(c) McLaren, L.M. 2003. "Anti-immigrant prejudice in Europe: Contact, threat perception, and preferences for the exclusion of migrants." *Social Forces*:909–936.

4 Research Design

4.1 OVERVIEW

As was the case in Chapter 3, there will not be any computer-based lessons in SPSS. Again, we offer some expanded exercises that will apply the lessons learned in the main text.

4.2 EXERCISES

1. There are a lot of substantive problems in social science that we might *wish* to study experimentally, but which might seem to be impossible to study with experimental methods. (Recall from the main text (Section 4.2.3) that one of the drawbacks to conducting experiments is that not all X variables are subject to experimental control and random assignment.) Imagine the following causal questions, and write a paragraph about what would be required to conduct an experiment in that particular research situation, being careful to refer to both halves of the two-part definition of an experiment in your answer. (Warning: Some of them will seem impossible, or nearly impossible, or might require time travel.)

   (a) Does an individual's religiosity cause a person's level of opposition to same-sex marriage?

   (b) Does a country's openness to trade cause blue-collar workers' wages to fall?

   (c) Does having a more racially diverse set of school administrators and teachers cause a reduction in student suspensions and expulsions?

   (d) Does race cause differences between African American and white girls' experiences in the science classroom?

2. For each of the above research situations, if you were *unable* to perform an experiment, name at least one Z variable that could potentially confound the $X–Y$ relationship, and would need to be controlled for in some other manner, in an observational study.

3. Assuming that you were unable to conduct an experiment for the aforementioned research situations, describe an observational study that you might conduct instead. In each case, is the study you envision a cross-sectional or time-series observational study? Why?

4. Consider the following research question: Does exposure to stories in the news media shape an individual's opinions on race- and/or gender-related policy issues (e.g., national policies on college admissions, hiring and promoting policies, etc.)?

   (a) Write a short paragraph trying to explain the causal mechanism that might be at work here.

   (b) If we wanted to study this relationship using an experiment, what would the barriers to conducting the experiment be?

   (c) What, if any, are the ethical considerations involved in studying that relationship experimentally?

   (d) What are the benefits of exploring that relationship experimentally? In other words, what specific Z variables would be controlled for in an experiment that could potentially be confounding in an observational study?

   (e) Read the following article and write a one-paragraph summary of it: King, G., Schneer, B., and White, A. 2017. "How the news media activate public expression and influence national agendas." *Science* 358:776–780.

5. Consider the relationship between the level of democracy in a country and the country's respect for human rights.

   (a) Describe both a cross-sectional and a time-series observational design that would help test the theory that increases in the level of democracy cause a country to increase its respect for human rights.

   (b) What concerns would you have about crossing the four causal hurdles in each case?

6. Write a one-paragraph summary of the following research articles:

   (a) Branton, R.P., and Jones, B.S. 2005. "Reexamining racial attitudes: The conditional relationship between diversity and socioeconomic environment." *American Journal of Political Science* 49(2):359–372.

(b) Sullivan, J.M., and Ghara, A. 2015. "Racial identity and intergroup attitudes: A multiracial youth analysis." *Social Science Quarterly* 96(1): 261–272.

(c) Bansak, K., Hainmueller, J., and Hangartner, D. 2016. "How economic, humanitarian, and religious concerns shape European attitudes toward asylum seekers." *Science* 354(6309):217–222.
In writing your summaries, address the following questions:

i. What was the research question/puzzle examined by the author(s)?

ii. What was their theory?

iii. What was their research design?

iv. How did they do with the four hurdles?

v. What did they conclude?

5 Survey Research

OVERVIEW

As was the case in Chapters 3 and 4, there will not be any computer-based lessons in SPSS. Again, we offer some expanded exercises that will apply the lessons learned in the main text.

5.2 EXERCISES

1. Select two articles from a social science journal that examine similar topics in an area of research interest to you, one that employs an experimental design and another that uses an observational design.

   (a) Provide a summary of each article, including a description of the dependent variable, the independent variable(s), and any Z variables. What is the primary causal mechanism, according to the authors, that links the independent and dependent variables? Which study do you think provides a more compelling answer to the research question?

   (b) Would it be feasible to combine the experimental and observational designs of the two studies that you selected in an effort to improve upon each?

2. In Exercise 5 in Chapter 5 of *FSR*, we asked you to describe a research question that you might be interested in examining using either the GSS or ANES data sets. We then asked you to describe how that research question might be expanded by using either the ISSP or WVS data sets. In this exercise, visit the website of either the GSS or ANES and the website of either the ISSP or WVS, depending on your selections in Chapter 5. Download to your computer the codebooks for the two data sets that you chose, and identify the variables that you would use to measure your key concepts.

6 Measuring Concepts of Interest

OVERVIEW

As was the case in Chapters 3, 4, and 5, there will not be any computer-based lessons in SPSS. Again, we offer some expanded exercises that will apply the lessons learned in the main text.

EXERCISES

1. Consider, for a moment, the concept of "customer satisfaction." For now, let's define it as "the degree to which a product or service meets or exceeds a customer's expectations." So, like other concepts, it is a variable: Some customers are very satisfied, some have mixed experiences, and some are very unhappy. Companies – and even some government agencies – are interested for obvious reasons in understanding that variation. Now answer the following questions:

   (a) How well do you think Yelp reviews serve as a measure of customer satisfaction? Explain your answer.

   (b) Read "The Happiness Button" in the February 5, 2018 issue of *The New Yorker*: www.newyorker.com/magazine/2018/02/05/customer-satisfaction-at-the-push-of-a-button. What are the strengths and weaknesses of the strategy pursued by HappyOrNot in terms of measuring the concept of customer satisfaction?

   (c) The article describes the push-button measures of satisfaction at security checkpoints in London's Heathrow Airport. What are the strengths and weaknesses of such an approach? If, on a particular day, there was a higher share of "frown" responses, what would that tell (and what wouldn't that tell) to the officials at Heathrow?

2. The concept of "religiosity" is a very important one in sociology, as it lies at the heart of many influential theories of why citizens hold the opinions that they do, including views of racial/ethnic minorities and homosexuality, and why they vote the way that they do. Answer the following questions:

   (a) Conceptually, how would you define religiosity? Try to be as specific as possible.

   (b) Measuring religiosity, as you might imagine, can be a bit tricky. The flagship specialty journal in the area of the sociology of religion is the *Journal for the Scientific Study of Religion* (hereafter *JSSR*). Go to the website for *JSSR* and search for articles that include "religiosity" in their titles. Read several of them, beginning with the most recent ones and working your way back to earlier issues of the journal. Make a list of the various questions that the authors use in their operational definitions of religiosity and the rationales that they use for doing so. Can you think of an alternative measurement strategy for this concept?

3. The concept of "consumer confidence" is important in the study of economics and political science, among other disciplines.

   (a) Go to https://news.google.com and search for "consumer confidence" (and be sure to use the quotation marks). From the search results, pick a recent news article that discusses consumer confidence. (Print out the article and include it with your homework.) How well, if at all, does the article define consumer confidence, or how it is measured?

   (b) From what you know, offer a conceptual definition of consumer confidence.

   (c) There are two major surveys in the U.S. that measure consumer confidence on monthly intervals. One of them is the Survey of Consumers at the University of Michigan. They produce what they call an Index of Consumer Sentiment, which is composed of responses to five survey items. One of the five is as follows:

   > Looking ahead, which would you say is more likely – that in the country as a whole we'll have continuous good times during the next five years or so, or that we will have periods of widespread unemployment or depression, or what?

   What are the potential strengths and weaknesses of this survey question as one component of consumer confidence?

   (d) All five of the items in the Michigan Index of Consumer Sentiment can be found here: https://data.sca.isr.umich.edu/fetchdoc.php?docid=24770. How are the five items similar to one another, and how are they different from one another?

(e) The complete monthly survey can be found here: https://data.sca .isr.umich.edu/fetchdoc.php?docid=24776. You will note that the survey does not contain *any* questions to measure a survey respondent's political beliefs or affiliations. Why do you think that is the case?

(f) Can you think of any additional survey questions that might complement or replace the ones in the Michigan Index?

7 Getting to Know Your Data

7.1 OVERVIEW

In this chapter we introduce you to the commands needed to produce descriptive statistics and graphs using SPSS. If you're feeling a little rusty on the basics of SPSS that we covered in Chapters 1 and 2, it would be good to review them before diving into this chapter.

In Chapter 7 of *FSR* we discussed a variety of tools that can be used to get to know your data one variable at a time. In this chapter, we discuss how to produce output in SPSS to allow you to get to know your variables. An important first step to getting to know your data is to figure out what is the measurement metric for each variable. For categorical and ordinal variables, we suggest producing frequency tables. For continuous variables, there are a wide range of descriptive statistics and graphs.

7.2 DESCRIBING CATEGORICAL AND ORDINAL VARIABLES

As we discussed in Chapter 7 of *FSR*, a frequency table is often the best way to numerically examine and present the distribution of values for a categorical or ordinal variable. We will learn to do this using one of the data sets from the main text, the 2014 General Social Survey.

As is our practice, the data are located in the directory "FSRSPSSFiles" on the computer that created this workbook. To navigate to that folder, we use the pull-down menus – "File" then "Open" then "Data" – and then change the drive and directory as necessary until we find the correct location where the data set is stored. The data file is called "GSS2014_New_Chap7.sav." Once you've found it, open it.

Table 7.1 in *FSR* shows a frequency distribution for the variable representing an individual respondent's religious identification. In SPSS,

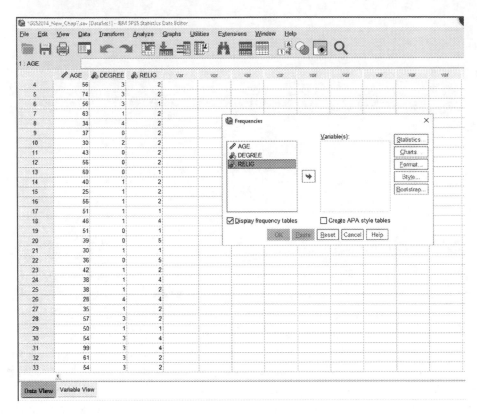

Figure 7.1 The dialog box of SPSS's Frequencies command

we generate this frequency distribution using the pull-down menu through clicking "Analyze," then "Descriptive Statistics," then "Frequencies. . . ." That will open a dialog box where we will choose which variables from the data set to analyze. A screenshot of that dialog box appears in Figure 7.1. The list of available variables to analyze – only three in this case – are on the left part of the dialog box. Hover your mouse over those variables to see their descriptions. The third of those, as you will discover, represents an individual's religious identification. Click on that, and then on the arrow button in the middle of the dialog box to select it. The variables in the right-hand box are the ones that will be analyzed.

We could click on the far right of the dialog box to select any statistics we'd like to see, to get a chart of the variables we analyze, and to edit the format and style of the results. More on this shortly. For now, however, just click "OK" and let's see the results.

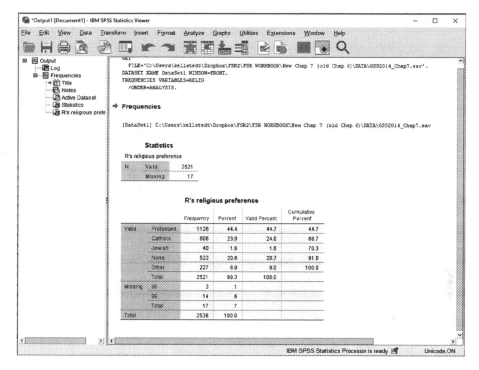

Figure 7.2 SPSS output of the Frequencies command

Figure 7.2 shows the screenshot of the SPSS output. The figure contains several columns of information. The far-left column presents the numeric values and their associated labels for each respondent's religious group – Protestant, Catholic, Jewish, None, and Other.[1] The next column, labeled "Frequencies," contains the raw number of cases – in this case, individual people who responded to the survey – in each category; so, for example, you can see that 1126 of the survey respondents identified as Protestant. The next column over, labeled "Percent," contains the percentage of all cases in each category; you can see that 44.4 percent of all cases identified as Protestant. Looking further down, you'll also notice that 0.7 percent are categorized as "Missing." Generally, that represents people in a survey who didn't know the answer to the question, or simply refused to answer. Because we generally don't want such cases to be part of our computations, the next column over is the "Valid Percent" – that is, the percentage of cases who chose one of the categories in the list of options. You'll notice that 44.7 percent of respondents who answered the question identified as Protestant. The final column represents the "Cumulative Percent," which is the percentage of cases with that particular value or lower.

---

[1] For purposes of illustration we include only these religious affiliations here.

(In this particular case, that is a meaningless calculation, because religious identification is a categorical variable that cannot be meaningfully ordered.)

Now take a moment to compare the table in Figure 7.2 with Table 7.1 of *FSR*. Although both tables convey the same information, Table 7.1 of *FSR* does so in a more polished fashion. This is an example of why we don't want to copy from the SPSS output and paste that into our papers or presentations. It's worth noting that you can, as is the case with most output in SPSS, right-click in the table, and copy and paste it into a word processing program. But we hope that looking at that output shows why that's not a particularly good idea. The extra columns of output might be of interest to the analyst – you might care how many people refused to answer the question and became "missing" data – but they are almost certainly not of interest to your audience. Instead, it is important to craft tables so that they convey what is most necessary and don't include a lot of extra information. We'll have more to say about making tables in Chapter 9 (and forward) in this workbook.

Pie graphs, such as Figure 7.1 in *FSR*, are a graphical way to get to know categorical and ordinal variables. In SPSS, we can get a pie chart

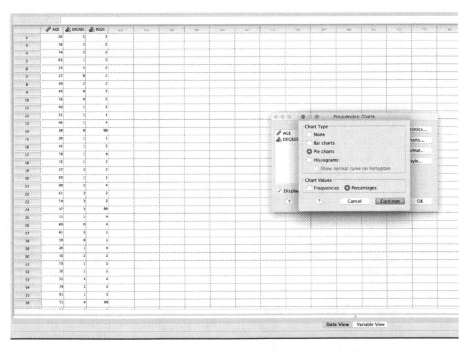

Figure 7.3 Obtaining a pie chart in SPSS as part of the Frequencies command

for our variable by using the same "Analyze," "Descriptive Statistics," "Frequencies..." procedure, and clicking on "Charts" to the right of that dialog box. It will open yet another dialog box like that presented in Figure 7.3, where we could select the radio button for "Pie charts." We could choose to have numeric values displayed as either raw frequencies or percentages. Once we've made our choice, click "Continue" and then "OK," and we'll see a pie chart in the output window. It looks nearly identical to the one in Figure 7.1 of *FSR*, though the legend is formatted and located differently. (As before, Figure 7.1 in the main text was generated using a different software program.) We can double-click on the graph to edit it if we choose to. We might prefer a different caption than the output provides, or none at all (in which case we could add a caption in our word processing software).

As you might guess, if we wanted a bar graph akin to the one in Figure 7.2 in *FSR*, we would just choose "Bar charts" instead of "Pie charts" in the dialog box for chart selection.

As we discuss is Chapter 7 of *FSR*, statisticians strongly prefer bar graphs to pie charts because bar graphs make it easier to make assessments about the relative frequency of different values.

7.3 DESCRIBING CONTINUOUS VARIABLES

While the values for categorical variables in a sample of data can easily be presented in a frequency table, this is usually not the case for continuous variables. Consider Table 7.2 in *FSR*, which contains 19 cases (each of which represents the percentage of African Americans who reported owning their home in the 1985 to 2014 General Social Surveys). Even for a relatively small data set such as this, the frequencies of each outcome in this output would be rather unwieldy. For this reason, we turn to summary statistics when we want to describe continuous variables. To use a metaphor, with summary statistics, we are looking at the broad contours of the forest rather than examining each individual tree.

To practice, let's use this same data set. As always, the data are located in the directory "FSRSPSSFiles" on the computer that created this workbook. To navigate to that folder, we use the pull-down menus – "File" then "Open" then "Data" – and then change the drive and directory as necessary until we find the correct location where the data set is stored. The data file is called "AA_Home-Ownership_1985-2014.sav." Once you've found it, open it.[2]

---

[2] Again, all of the data sets we use can be found in the SPSS directory at www.cambridge.org/fsr.

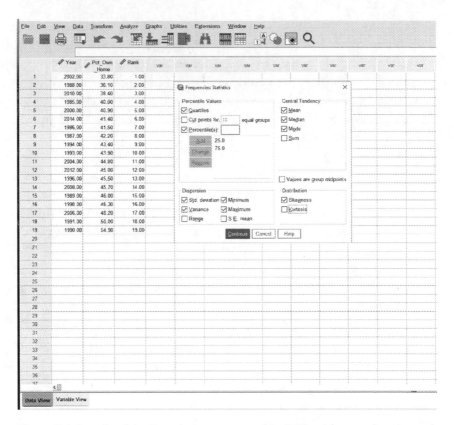

Figure 7.4 Details of the Descriptives command in SPSS, with several options selected

Figure 7.3 in *FSR* displays a full battery of descriptive statistics for the continuous variable *Home Ownership* (which we named "Pct_Own_Home" in the data set). We obtain SPSS's equivalent of that information by using the pull-down menu under "Analyze," "Descriptive Statistics," and then "Frequencies...," which opens up the familiar dialog box, and select variables as before. On the right of the dialog box, we choose the "Statistics" option to choose what statistics SPSS will generate for us.

As you see in our screenshot in Figure 7.4, there's a good number of options. And if you're a bit overwhelmed by the choices, perhaps you feel tempted to just check all of the boxes and figure out what information you need later on. (We've seen our students do that many times in our lab sessions!) You'll see from the detail in Figure 7.4 that we've selected many (but not all) of those options. Clicking "Continue" and then "OK" gets you the output. From the discussion in Chapter 7 of *FSR*, we can see that this command presents both rank statistics and moment statistics to describe the values taken on by continuous variables.

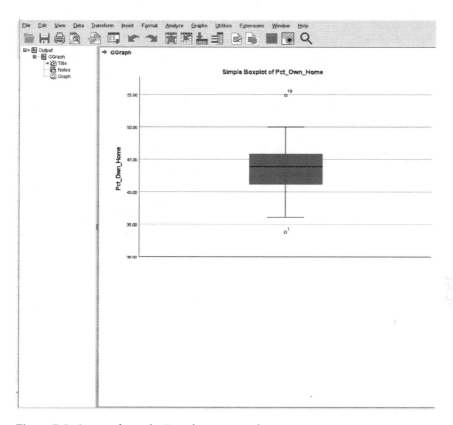

Figure 7.5 Output from the Boxplot command

While statistical summaries of variables are helpful, it is also some-times informative to look at visual summaries of the values for a variable. To get a visual depiction of rank statistics, we recommend producing a box–whisker plot like that displayed in Figure 7.4 in *FSR*. We make that chart using SPSS's Chart Builder, like we learned in Chapter 2 of this workbook. We begin by using the pull-down menu and selecting "Graphs" followed by "Chart Builder. . . ." That opens up the Chart Builder dialog box, and, from there, we begin in the lower-left portion, and click on "Boxplot" from the "Gallery" tab. Then double-click "Simple Boxplot," which activates the chart preview in the pane above. From the variable list in the top left, grab and drag "Pct_Own_Home" onto the Y (vertical) axis of the chart preview area. Then click "OK" to see our box–whisker plot.

Figure 7.5 displays SPSS's first attempt, and it's not bad. But we hope that you're growing accustomed to looking at these graphs with a critical eye, and a few details stand out to us as less than ideal. For example, that pesky title that we didn't ask for – "Simple Boxplot of Pct_Own_Home" – across the top. As you can imagine, we can change this in the output window by double-clicking on the box–whisker plot and

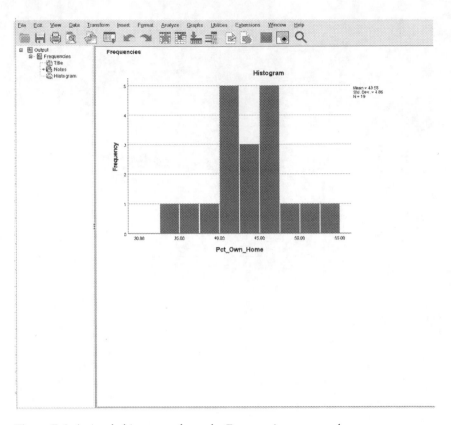

Figure 7.6 A simple histogram from the Frequencies command

then single-clicking on the title, then pressing the "Delete" key, and editing the *Y* axis by double-clicking on that, and using our mouse and keyboard to edit the text into a more meaningful label.

To get a visual depiction of moment statistics, we recommend producing a histogram as in Figure 7.5 from *FSR*. We can obtain a simple histogram from the Frequencies command ("Analyze," "Descriptive Statistics," and then "Frequencies...") by clicking the "Charts" option and then selecting the radio button for "Histograms."

Figure 7.6 displays the resulting graph. Again, it's not bad, though if you wish you can edit this, as we've just described, by double-clicking on the chart in the output window. As before, this histogram generated by SPSS differs slightly from the one in *FSR*, which was produced using a different software package.

In this version of histograms, SPSS makes all of the decisions about the width of the bins for you. In case you'd like more control over the process, you can use the "Chart Builder" process that you've become familiar with, beginning with the "Histogram" option from the "Gallery" tab on the lower left part of the dialog box, and then double-clicking "Simple Histogram" from among the options. You would grab, drag, and drop the "Pct_Own_Home" variable onto the X axis. Customizing the bin widths happens by clicking on the "Element Properties" tab on the far right of the dialog box, then clicking the "Bar1" option under the "Edit Properties of" window. The button "Set Parameters" will open another dialog box, and then you can customize the bin width under the "Bin Sizes" portion of that window.

7.4 PUTTING STATISTICAL OUTPUT INTO TABLES, DOCUMENTS, AND PRESENTATIONS

So you've generated some statistical output for the first time. Congratulations! But now what do you do? As you can tell from the descriptions above, we think it's important to be thoughtful about how to present your results to your audience. That's why we went to great lengths to show you commands to make the graphics appear in the most interpretable way possible. The same is true with data that you wish to include in a tabular format. We emphasize that just copying and pasting output from SPSS (or any other program) is unlikely to impress your audience – even if your audience is "just" your professor or teaching assistant.

For example, when we produce descriptive statistics in SPSS using the commands we described above, we tend to get a *lot* of output. Usually this output is much more than what we need to present in a paper that describes our variables one at a time. We therefore suggest making your own tables in whatever word processing program you are working with.

Graphs are a bit simpler, though. Once you have a graph that meets the standards we've outlined above, and you want to include in a document, one of the easiest ways to do so is to right-click on the graph in SPSS and select "copy" and then right-click on the location where you want to place the graph in your word processing program and select "paste." Depending on the word processor, you might just want to resize the graphic image by clicking on the corner of the image and dragging the image to be bigger or smaller, depending on what would look best in your paper or presentation.

We'll have more to say about this topic in Chapter 9, and forward, as we introduce new statistical techniques to you. The upshot, though, is always the same: Put some care into what you present to your audience. The amount of attention you devote to the details – great or small – will be obvious to your audience.

7.5 EXERCISES

1. Launch SPSS and open the "GSS2014_New_Chap7.sav" data set. Once you have done this, follow the procedures described in this workbook chapter to produce the graphs presented in Figures 7.1 and 7.2 from *FSR*. Open a word processing document and then copy these figures from SPSS and paste them into your word processing document.

2. Using the same dataset, run a Frequencies command for variable "degree," which is respondents' highest education degree received. In your word processing document, create a professional-looking frequency table like Table 7.1 from *FSR* for variable "degree."

3. Create a pie chart and a bar graph like Figures 7.1 and 7.2 from *FSR* for variable "degree." Copy these figures from SPSS and paste them into your word processing document.

4. Write a short summary of what you see in the table and figures that you created using variable "degree."

5. Using the same "GSS2014_New_Chap7.sav" data set, follow the procedures described in this workbook chapter to create a box–whisker plot and a histogram for the variable "age." Copy and paste each of these figures into your word processing document.

6. Generate descriptive statistics for the variable "age." Make a table in your word processing document which contains the moment statistics for this variable.

7. Write a short summary of what you see in the table and figures that you created using variable "age."

8 Probability and Statistical Inference

8.1 OVERVIEW

In this chapter, we teach you how to use a computer simulation using a preprogrammed Excel spreadsheet. The goal of this chapter is to familiarize you with some of the basics of how probability works, and especially to see how sample sizes come into play.

8.2 DICE ROLLING IN EXCEL

There are a variety of free spreadsheets available online that simulate the rolling of dice.[1] The one we will use is available at the SPSS link at www.cambridge.org/fsr.

Right-click on the filename "diceroller.xls" and save it to your computer.[2] Find the file and open it. What you'll see should look like Figure 8.1.

The spreadsheet is quite simple: It contains a basic program that simulates the rolling of two six-sided dice, with a graphic display of the resulting dice faces, as well as output data to keep track of the rolls. The sheet basically contains three sections. In the top left of the sheet are the two dice. In the launch screen in Figure 8.1, those dice are a 5 and a 1. There are also buttons there to roll the dice – you can click the "Roll 'em (Ctr+R)" button or press "Ctrl" and "R" on your keyboard. You can click the "Clear History" button to erase the history of rolls and start over.

The history of rolls of the two dice are displayed along the lower-left side of the sheet. In that section, there are columns of data that correspond to the roll number ("Roll #"), the roll of die 1 ("D1"), the roll of die 2

---

[1] Google "spreadsheet dice roller" to find several of them.

[2] Unfortunately, the functionality of the spreadsheet only works in Microsoft Excel, so if you're used to using Google Sheets, you'll need to be on a computer that has Microsoft Excel installed on it.

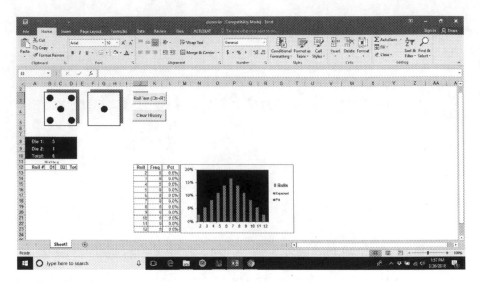

Figure 8.1 The dice roller in Excel

("D2"), and the sum of die 1 and die 2 ("Tot"). In Figure 8.1, since we haven't rolled the dice yet, you will see that in the rows beneath the display of "Roll #, D1, D2, Tot," the cells are all empty. When we begin rolling the dice, those rows will begin to fill up.

The third section of the sheet, in the lower right, shows the actual sum of the two dice (from the "Tot" column) – which will appear in red bars – as well as the distribution that we would *expect* to see given that the dice are fair – shown in gray bars.

Let's go ahead and roll the dice, either by hovering your mouse over the "Roll 'em" button and left-clicking it or hitting "Ctrl" and "R" on your keyboard. The results of our first roll are in Figure 8.2. As you can see, we rolled a "snake eyes" – a 1 and a 1. (Obviously, when you're doing this on your own computer, you might roll something different!) All of the output looks as you'd expect. In the lower left of the sheet, you see that, for roll 1, die 1 was a 1 and die 2 was also a 1, making the total (the sum) 2 (because 1 plus 1 equals 2). That's reflected in the graph on the lower-right portion of the sheet, with a large red bar at the spot for 2, indicating that all 100 percent of rolls so far totalled a 2.

Let's click "Roll 'em" a few more times, so that we get ten rolls in total.

Figure 8.3 shows the results of the first ten rolls that we performed when writing this chapter. (Again, the outcomes of your rolls are quite likely to be different than ours!) You'll notice from the figure that we haven't rolled another "snake eyes." In fact, we've rolled three 4s, two 6s, and the other five results just one apiece.

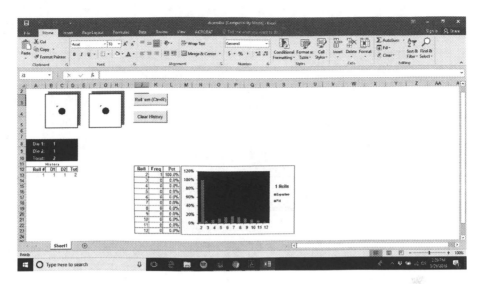

Figure 8.2 The results of our first roll

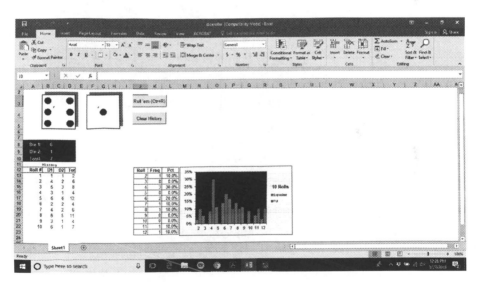

Figure 8.3 The results of our first ten rolls

We can roll the dice as many times as we'd like. (Just press "Ctrl" and "R" on your keyboard repeatedly. Yes, that means pressing it 100 times if you want 100 rolls, or 1000 times if you want 1000 rolls.) Go ahead and roll the dice around 100 times, and watch the red and gray bars shift as you do. (For our purposes right now, it doesn't matter if you roll them exactly 100 times.)

Figure 8.4 shows our results. As always, your rolls will be different from the ones we got. Let's examine the results in the figure. As you can see from the output screen and associated bar graph, we have rolled a total of

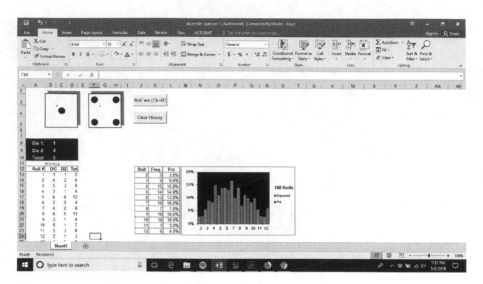

Figure 8.4 The results of our first 100 rolls

4 – either through a 1 and a 3, or a pair of 2s, or a 3 and a 1 – fifteen times out of 100. That's more than would be expected by chance. You can also see that we've managed to roll double-6s six times out of the 100 rolls – again, more than would be expected. Perhaps the biggest discrepancy between the observed outcomes in red and the expected ones in gray is in the rolls that total 8. For whatever reason, we rolled about half as many 8s as would have been expected by chance.

Let's be clear: None of the above is meant to imply a judgment – positive or negative – on what we've found. In theory, there are a "squadpillion" possible rolls of these two dice, and what we've just done is sample one, then ten, and then 100 of them. At the extreme, rolling the two dice just one time produced a rather odd – by definition! – "outcome." Every single roll (of that one roll!)was a 2! How weird is that? Of course, for a single roll, *any* outcome would have been "odd" in this sense. As we move from one roll to ten to 100, though, we start to see the beginning of convergence between what we observe and what we expect to observe. Will the observed outcomes ever *exactly* equal the expected ones? Probably not.

One other thing that Excel allows us to do is to calculate the averages of the rolls of the individual die, and of the dice collectively. Doing so is straightforward. For example, if we want to calculate the average of the rolls of die 1, we can go anywhere in the spreadsheet and type

```
=average(b13:b112)
```

and hit the "Enter" key on your keyboard. (You'll see that we performed this in cell b114, because it is below the bottom of the string of cells for which we are calculating the mean, with a single space in between the last

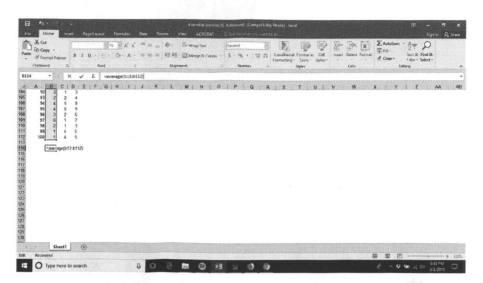

Figure 8.5 How to calculate the average of our first 100 rolls of die 1

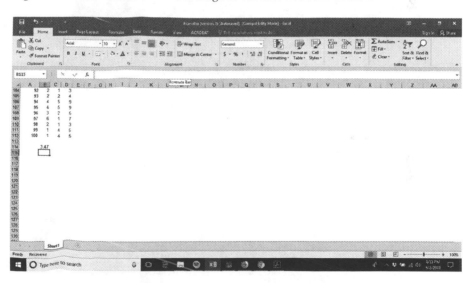

Figure 8.6 The result of calculating the average of our first 100 rolls of die 1

cell of data – cell b112 – and where we want our mean to be displayed.) That process is displayed in Figure 8.5, before we hit the "Enter" key. When we hit the "Enter" key, of course, the result will appear.

As you can see in Figure 8.6, the average of our 100 rolls of die 1 is 3.47. (We repeat the admonition that, when you perform this in your own spreadsheet, you will almost certainly get different results.) When we repeat the process – that is, type

```
=average(c13:c112)
```

in cell c114 – for die 2, we find a different result, as is evident in Figure 8.7.

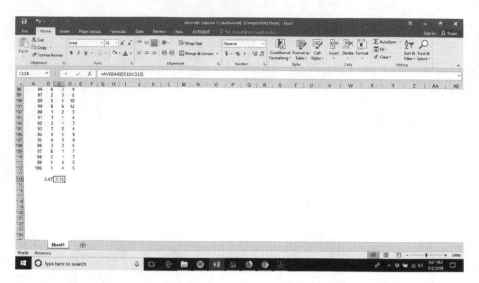

Figure 8.7 The result of calculating the average of our first 100 rolls of die 2

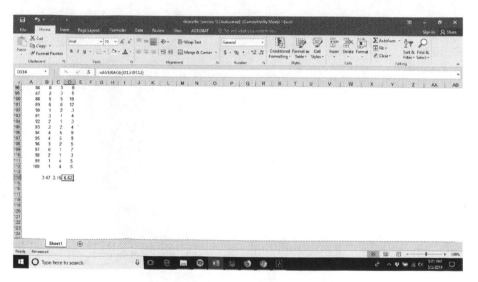

Figure 8.8 The result of calculating the average of our first 100 rolls of the sum of dice 1 and 2

That mean is 3.15. Does that figure seem "too low" to you? (And why did we type "too low" in scare quotes just there?) Obviously, in a mathematical sense, the result of 3.15 for die 2 is lower than the outcome of 3.47 for die 1: 3.15 < 3.47, we all know. We have computed the average of the sum of dice 1 and 2 in column D.

That result is displayed in Figure 8.8, and shows that the mean is 6.62. Because the mean of the rolls of die 1 is 3.47, and the mean of the rolls of die 2 is 3.15, the fact that the mean of the sum is 6.62 should not be surprising (3.47 + 3.15 = 6.62).

8.3 EXERCISES

1. In Figure 8.1 from the dice rolling module in Excel, before we actually roll any dice, what should we *expect* the mean of a set of rolls of a single die to be? Why? And what should we expect the mean of the sum of the rolls of two dice to be? Why? How do these numbers compare to the outcomes we found in Figures 8.6, 8.7, and 8.8?

2. In Figure 8.2, you notice that we happened to roll two 1s. Given that, what is the probability of rolling two 1s on the next roll? Explain your answer.

3. You've surely noticed that the gray bars in the dice rolling module in Excel – representing the "expected" rolls – in all of the dice figures seem to be shaped almost like a normal distribution. Why is that? Be careful in answering this question, and try to be as explicit as possible in arriving at your answer.

4. If you haven't already, in the dice rolling module in Excel, roll your dice 100 times. What are the means of die 1, die 2, and the sum of the two? How do these numbers compare to the outcomes we found in Figures 8.6, 8.7, and 8.8? What do you make of these similarities or differences?

5. Using the dice rolling module in Excel, roll the dice until the "observed" bars (in red) *roughly* approximate the gray "expected" bars. How many rolls did it take? Print out (or take a screenshot) of your output and turn it in with your answer.

9 Bivariate Hypothesis Testing

9.1 OVERVIEW

We are now ready to start testing hypotheses! As we discuss in Chapter 9 of *FSR*, bivariate hypothesis tests, or hypothesis tests carried out with only two variables, are seldom used as the primary means of hypothesis testing in social science research today. But it is imperative to understand the basic mechanics of bivariate hypothesis tests before moving to more complicated tests. This same logic applies to the use of statistical computing software. In this chapter, we teach you how to conduct hypothesis tests in SPSS using the four techniques presented in Chapter 9 of *FSR*: tabular analysis, difference of means, the correlation coefficient, and analysis of variance.

9.2 TABULAR ANALYSIS

In tabular analysis, we are testing the null hypothesis that the column variable and row variable are unrelated to each other. We will review the basics of producing a table in which the rows and columns are defined by the values of two different variables, generating hypothesis-testing statistics, and then presenting what you have found. We will learn to do this using the data sets from the main text, which include the 2014 General Social Survey – a survey of public opinion administered almost yearly between 1972 and 1994 and biennially since 1996.

As is our practice, the data are located in the directory "MyFSR-SPSSFiles" on the computer that created this workbook. To navigate to that folder, we use the pull-down menus – "File" then "Open" then "Data" – and then change the drive and directory as necessary until we find the correct location where the data set is stored. The data file is called "GSS2014_Sample_Chap9_v5.sav." Once you've found it, open it.[1]

---

[1] Depending upon which SPSS package (not version) you are using, you may be unable to precisely replicate some of the tables and figures in the main text using your computer's

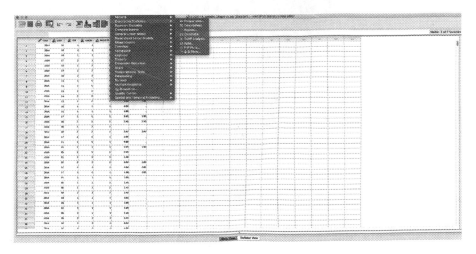

Figure 9.1 Navigating to SPSS's Crosstabs command

We produce a tabular analysis in SPSS by using the Crosstabs command, which we run by using the pull-down menu by clicking "Analyze," then "Descriptive Statistics," then "Crosstabs. . . ." That process is shown in Figure 9.1.

That will open a dialog box where we will choose which variables from the data set to analyze, shown in Figure 9.2. In that figure, you can see the list of variables available in the data set from which you can choose, and selection boxes for which variables we want in the rows and columns. As we note in Chapter 9 of *FSR*, it is customary to put your dependent variable into the "Row(s)" box and your independent variable into the "Column(s)" box.

As detailed in Chapter 9 of *FSR*, if we set up our independent and dependent variables like this, then column percentages allow for the comparison of interest – they tell us how the dependent variable values differ in terms of their distribution across values of the independent variable. It is crucial, when working with tables of this nature, to put the appropriate variables across the rows and columns of the table and then to

statistical software. Rather than making frequent trips to on-campus computer laboratories to do their assignments, some students prefer to rent or purchase the SPSS computer software package directly from IBM. The only downside for this convenience is that the most affordable of the SPSS software products are limited to a maximum of 1500 cases and 50 variables. While the variable limit is more than adequate for most students' purposes, the limit on the number of cases can be a problem. Many of the data sets routinely used by social scientists, including several that you will be using this semester, exceed 1500 cases. In an effort to provide students with the access necessary to master statistical computing, we have designed most of the exercises in Chapters 9 through 12 of this workbook to require no more than 1500 cases. You won't be disadvantaged by renting or purchasing your software this semester.

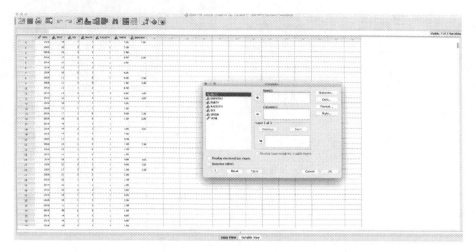

Figure 9.2 The dialog box for SPSS's Crosstabs command

present the column frequencies. (If you need a refresher on this, look at the tables in Figure 9.5 of the main text.)

For example, if we were to attempt to recreate Table 9.2 in *FSR*, we would click on "Union" in the variables list in the left-hand box, and click the arrow to place that variable into the "Column(s)" box, then click on "Party" and click the arrow to place that variable into the "Row(s)" box – where "Party" is a categorical variable that takes on a value of "1" if the respondent reported being a Democrat and "2" if the respondent reported being a Republican, and "Union" is a variable that takes on a value of "1" if the respondent reported that someone in their household belonged to a union and "2" otherwise. In order to obtain column percentages, we click on the "Cells…" box on the right-hand side of the dialog box, and under "Percentages," check "Column." Then click "Continue" and then "OK" at the bottom of the Crosstabs dialog box.

The output from this example is displayed in Figure 9.3. Take a moment to compare this raw output with Table 9.2 in *FSR*. There are three notable differences. First, as we noted at the beginning of the chapter, this analysis is being conducted on a sample of the data, whereas the table in the main text is based on the complete data set, so the percentages differ slightly. Second, in order to isolate the numbers needed for the assessment at hand (whether or not respondents from union households are different from those in nonunion households in terms of party affiliation), in Table 9.2 of the main text we only present the column percentages. Third, in the table in *FSR*, we have added a note making it clear what are the values reported in each cell of the table.

A note of caution: In the "Cells…" box, you'll notice that there are a *lot* of choices. What would happen if – say, because you happened to

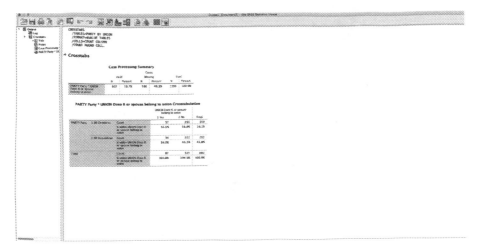

Figure 9.3 Raw output from SPSS's Crosstabs command

forget which type of information you want in your cells – you checked them all? The resulting table would be a frightening mess, containing way too much information, which would obscure the actual pattern you sought to discover. Just for fun, you can go ahead and try it. You'll see.

9.2.1 Generating Test Statistics

In Chapter 9 of *FSR* we discuss in detail the logic of Pearson's chi-squared test statistic which we use to test the null hypothesis that the row and column variables are not related. To get this test statistic and the associated p-value for a two-variable table in SPSS, from the Crosstabs dialog box, we click the "Statistics..." box on the far right, and then check the "Chi-square" box in the top left of that new dialog box, and then click "Continue" (and "OK" to run the tabular analysis again).

That output is displayed in Figure 9.4. The calculated value of the chi-squared statistic is 2.274 – you could do it by hand following the formula in Chapter 9 of the main text – and the associated p-value is 0.132. Because that is greater than 0.05, the relationship is not statistically significant, meaning that it very likely does not exist in the underlying population from which the sample was drawn.

9.2.2 Putting Tabular Results into Papers

We recommend that you make your own tables in whatever word processing program you choose to use instead of copying and pasting the tables that you make in SPSS. The first reason for doing so is that you will think about your results more closely when you are producing your

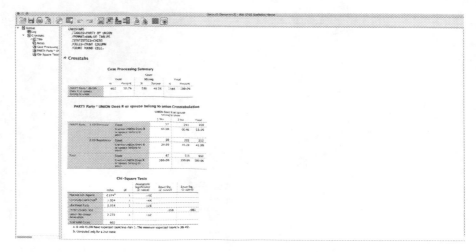

Figure 9.4 Obtaining the chi-squared statistic from SPSS's Crosstabs command

own tables. This will help you to catch any mistakes that you might have made and to write more effectively about what you have found. Another reason for doing so is that tables constructed by you will tend to look better. (By comparison, look at all of the clutter in the chi-squared test shown in Figure 9.4. Who wants all of that in their assignments, papers, and presentations?) By controlling how the tables are constructed, you will be able to communicate with maximum clarity.

As a part of making your own tables, you should have the goal in mind that your table communicates something on its own. In other words, if someone *only* looked at your table, would they be able to figure out what was going on? If the answer is "yes," then you have constructed an effective table. We offer the following advice ideas for making useful tables:

- Give your tables a title that conveys the essential result in your table.
- Make your column and row headings as clear as possible.
- Put notes at the bottom of your tables to explain the table's contents.

9.3 DIFFERENCE OF MEANS

As we show in Table 9.1 in *FSR*, difference of means tests are conducted when we have a continuous dependent variable and a categorical independent variable.

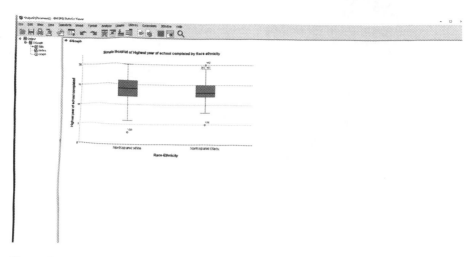

Figure 9.5 SPSS output of a box–whisker plot

9.3.1 Examining Differences Graphically

When we use graphs to assess a difference of means, we are graphing the distribution of the continuous dependent variable for two or more values of the limited independent variable. Figure 9.1 of *FSR* shows how this is done with box–whisker plots, which we learned to do in SPSS in Chapter 7 of this workbook. We will learn to do this using one of the data sets from the main text.

As is our practice, the data are located in the directory "FSRSPSSFiles" on the computer that created this workbook. To navigate to that folder, we use the pull-down menus – "File" then "Open" then "Data" – and then change the drive and directory as necessary until we find the correct location where the data set is stored. The data file is called "GSS2014_Sample_Chap9_v5.sav." Once you've found it, open it.

As a reminder of what we learned in Chapter 7, we make the box–whisker plots using SPSS's Chart Builder. We begin by using the pull-down menu and selecting "Graphs" followed by "Chart Builder...." That opens up the Chart Builder dialog box, and, from there, we begin in the lower-left portion, and click on "Boxplot" from the "Gallery" tab. Then double-click "Simple Boxplot," which activates the chart preview in the pane above. From the variable list in the top left, grab and drag "Educ" onto the Y (vertical) axis of the chart preview area, and grab and drag the variable "Raceeth" onto the X (horizontal) axis. Then click "OK" to see our box–whisker plot.

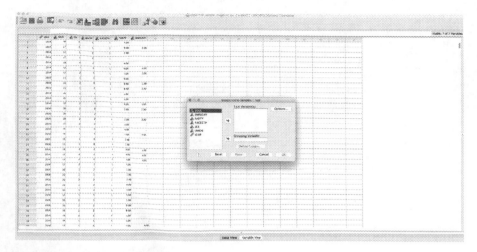

Figure 9.6 The independent *t*-test dialog box menu in SPSS

Figure 9.5 displays our resulting box–whisker plot, and it's quite similar to Figure 9.1 in the main text. (The one in the main text was generated with a different software program.) As we learned in Chapter 7, it's easy to edit these graphs to add or remove details to our axes, for example.

9.3.2 Generating Test Statistics

To conduct a difference of means *t*-test such as the one discussed in Chapter 9 of *FSR*, we navigate through the pull-down menus by clicking "Analyze," then "Compare Means," then "Independent-Samples T Test...," which opens up a dialog box like the one pictured in Figure 9.6. Our dependent variable, which must be continuous, is the "Highest year of school completed" variable, so we click "Educ" from our variable list on the left and use the arrow key to insert it into the "Test Variable(s)" box. Our independent variable is the variable "Race_Ethnicity," so we click that into the "Grouping Variable" box using the arrow. We then have to define the groups, so click on the "Define Groups..." button, which opens another dialog box. Our values for that variable are 1 and 2, so type those (respectively) into the boxes for Group 1 (Nonhispanic Whites) and Group 2 (Nonhispanic Blacks), then click "Continue," and then "OK" to run the analysis.

The output appears in Figure 9.7. You will note there that it provides the means and standard deviations, followed by the *t*-test calculation. The calculated $t = 3.778$, which is statistically significant ($p < 0.001$).

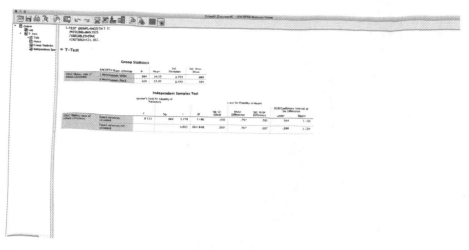

Figure 9.7 Output from the independent *t*-test

9.4 CORRELATION COEFFICIENTS

Correlation coefficients summarize the relationship between two continuous variables. They are also an important building block to understanding the basic mechanics of two-variable regression models.

To practice calculating correlation coefficients, let's use the data set on the state of the economy (as measured by the unemployment rate) and support for assistance to the poor. As always, the data are located in the directory "FSRSPSSFiles" on the computer that created this workbook. To navigate to that folder, we use the pull-down menus – "File" then "Open" then "Data" – and then change the drive and directory as necessary until we find the correct location where the data set is stored. The data file is called "GovtAsst.sav." Once you've found it, open it.

9.4.1 Producing Scatter Plots

We can examine the relationship between two continuous variables in a scatter plot such as Figure 9.2 in *FSR*, which displays the relationship between the unemployment rate and citizen support for government assistance to the poor.

We make the scatter plot using SPSS's Chart Builder. We begin by using the pull-down menu and selecting "Graphs" followed by "Chart Builder...." That opens up the Chart Builder dialog box, and, from there, we begin in the lower-left portion, and click on "Scatter/Dot" from the "Gallery" tab. Then double-click "Simple Scatter," which activates the

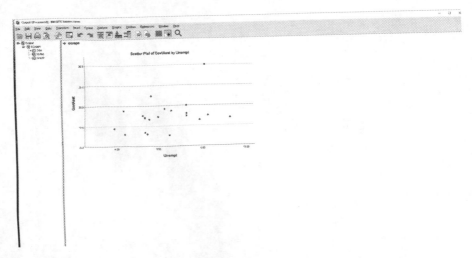

Figure 9.8 Output from a scatter plot

chart preview in the pane above. From the variable list in the top left, grab and drag "GovtAsst" onto the Y (vertical) axis of the chart preview area, and grab and drag the variable "Unempl" onto the X (horizontal) axis. Then click "OK" to see our scatter plot.

The result is displayed in Figure 9.8, and you'll see a striking resemblance between that and Figure 9.2 in the main text. As before, there might be details that we'd like to edit for purposes of turning in assignments, writing papers, or making presentations – especially about titles and axis labels. You can edit those by double-clicking on the graph in the output window and editing away as we showed you in Chapter 2 of this workbook.

9.4.2 Generating Correlation Coefficients and Test Statistics

To obtain a correlation coefficient like the one in Section 9.4.3 in *FSR*, we use the pull-down menu and click "Analyze," then "Correlate," then "Bivariate...," which will open up a simple dialog box. We simply click the variables there for which we want to produce the correlations, and use the right arrow to add them to the "Variables" window on the right-hand side.[2] You'll see that the "Pearson" box is checked by default – if it is not, go ahead and check it – and then click "OK."

The output is displayed in Figure 9.9. You'll see that SPSS produces a correlation matrix, which shows the correlations across all pairs of variables. So, for example, "GovtAsst" correlates at exactly 1 with itself,

---

[2] If we would like to compute the covariance table like Table 9.10 in the main text, that can be checked under "Options."

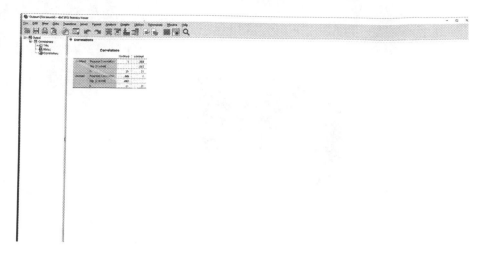

Figure 9.9 Output from the SPSS Correlate command

and the same is true of "Unempl." (Hopefully, that's intuitive.) The correlation between "GovtAsst" and "Unempl" is 0.389, which (except for rounding) is the same number we calculated in Section 9.4.3 in the main text. SPSS also reports, in the row "Sig. (2-tailed)," that the p-value for this correlation coefficient is 0.082, which means that the relationship is not statistically significant at the 0.05 level.

9.5 ANALYSIS OF VARIANCE

Our final example of bivariate hypothesis testing is analysis of variance, or ANOVA for short. As Table 9.1 in *FSR* shows, ANOVA models, like difference of means tests, require a continuous dependent variable and a categorical independent variable. However, as we discuss in Section 9.4.4 of the main text, ANOVA, unlike difference of means tests, is appropriate when the independent variable has three or more, rather than two, categories.

9.5.1 Examining Differences Graphically

As we did earlier in this chapter (Section 9.3.2) for a continuous dependent variable and an independent variable with two categories, in this section we illustrate how to graphically analyze a continuous dependent variable and an independent variable with three categories. The data set we use is "GSS2014_Sample_Chap9_ANOVA.sav". As usual, the data are located in the "FSRSPSSFiles" folder on the computer that created this workbook. To navigate to that folder again, use the pull-down menus – "File" th

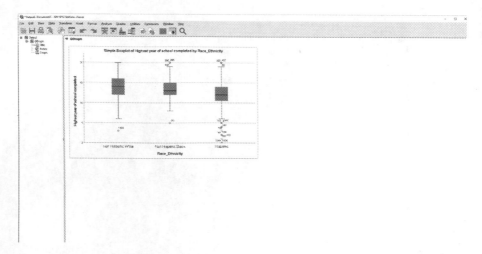

Figure 9.10 Box–whisker plot of racial/ethnic differences in education

"Open" then "Data" – and change the drive and directory as necessary to locate the data set. Once you've found it, open it.

In order to replicate the box–whisker plots in Figure 9.10 in this workbook, simply repeat the steps that you followed in Section 9.3.1. As a reminder, begin by using the pull-down menu and selecting "Graphs" followed by "Chart Builder...." That opens up the Chart Builder dialog box, and, from there, begin in the lower-left portion and click on "Boxplot" from the "Gallery" tab. Then double-click "Simple Boxplot," which activates the chart preview in the pane above. From the variable list in the top left, grab and drag "Educ" onto the Y (vertical) axis of the chart preview area, and grab and drag the variable "Race_Ethnicity" onto the X (horizontal) axis. Then click "OK" to see our box–whisker plot. Figure 9.10 displays the results. As before, you can easily edit the graph to your liking.

9.5.2 Generating ANOVA Test Statistics

To conduct an analysis of variance test such as the one discussed in Chapter 9 of *FSR*, click "Analyze," then "Compare Means," then "One-Way ANOVA...," which opens up a dialog box like the one pictured in *Figure* 9.11. Our dependent variable, which must be continuous, is "Highest year of school completed," so we click "Educ" from our variable list on the left and use the arrow key to insert it into the "Dependent List" window. Our independent variable is the categorical "Race_Ethnicity" variable, which we highlight and place into the "Factor" window.

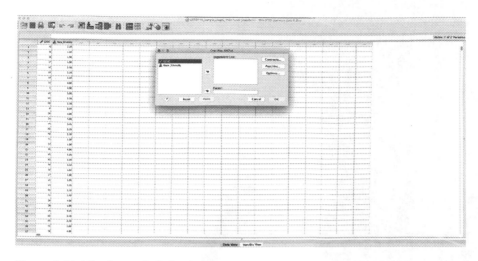

Figure 9.11 The ANOVA dialog box menu in SPSS

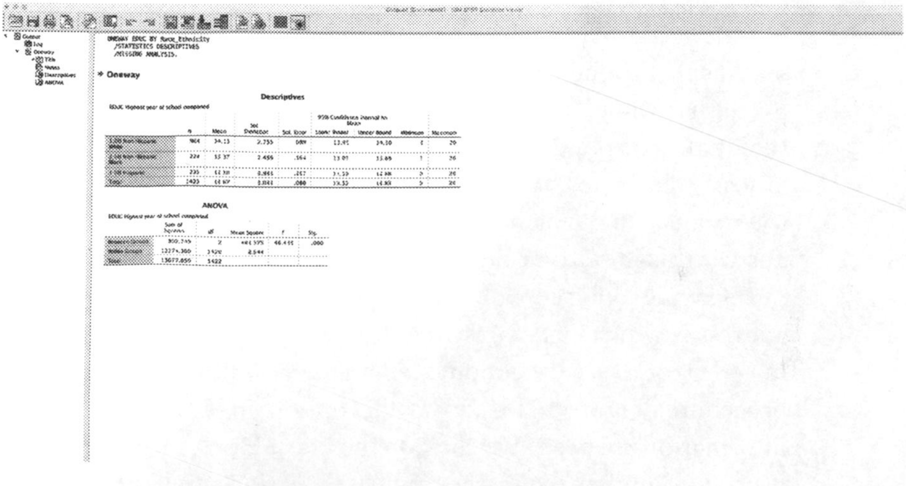

Figure 9.12 Output from an ANOVA analysis in SPSS

the arrow. Next, click on the "Options" tab, highlight "Descriptives" in the "Statistics" window, and then "Continue." Click "OK" to run the analysis.

The output appears in Figure 9.12. In the "Descriptives" panel of the output file, several descriptive statistics for each of our three groups – Non-Hispanic Whites, Non-Hispanic Blacks, and Hispanics – are reported. A look at the entries in the column labeled "Mean" shows the average number of years of education completed for each group. Are these means large enough to warrant rejection of our null hypothesis of no racial/ethnic group differences in educational attainment in the underlying population?

Figure 9.13 The multiple comparison dialog box

To answer this question, we must look at the ANOVA panel of output – specifically, to the last column of that panel where the p-value is reported. Since that value, 0.000, is less than 0.05, we can reject the null hypothesis of equality of population means in favor of the alternative hypothesis that at least one mean (or means) is (are) different from at least one other mean (or means). But which ones are different from which others? In order to answer this important question, we have to take one additional step.

Having rejected our null hypothesis, the final question we need to address is which mean(s) is (are) different from which other mean or means. In order to do so, we conduct what is referred to as a multiple comparison procedure. Figure 9.13 shows the option in ANOVA that provides the information we need. We click on the "Post Hoc..." button in the ANOVA procedure and then on the "Scheffe" option, and then "Continue" and "OK." The results are displayed in Figure 9.14.

An examination of Figure 9.14 shows that each of the group means is significantly different from each of the other group means. In other words, non-Hispanic whites have significantly higher educational attainment than both non-Hispanic blacks and Hispanics; non-Hispanic blacks have significantly lower educational attainment than non-Hispanic whites but significantly higher educational attainment than Hispanics; and Hispanics are significantly lower on educational attainment than both whites and blacks.[3]

---

[3] You can ignore the "Homogeneous Subsets" part of the output; it need not concern us here.

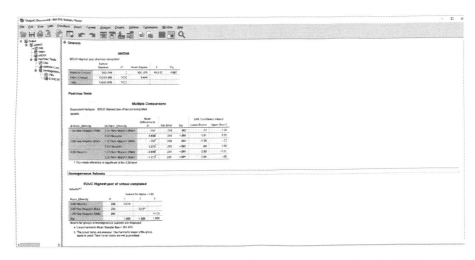

Figure 9.14 Output from an ANOVA multiple comparison procedure in SPSS

9.6 EXERCISES

1. Launch SPSS and open the "GSS2014_Sample_Chap9_v5.sav" data set. Once you have done this, conduct a chi-squared test of the null hypothesis that sex and party are statistically independent. Discuss your results.

2. Using the same data set, perform a difference of means test using sex as the independent variable and education as the dependent variable. Discuss your results.

3. Launch SPSS and open the "GovtAsst.sav" data set. Once you have done this, output a correlation matrix showing the relationship between unemployment rate and attitudes toward government assistance toward the poor. Discuss your results.

4. Launch SPSS and open "GSS2014_Sample_Exercises_Chap9.sav." Perform an analysis of variance to determine whether Protestants, Catholics, and those with no religious affiliation ("Nones") differ on age. If you reject the null hypothesis, perform a multiple comparison procedure to determine which religious groups differ from which others.

10 Two-Variable Regression Models

10.1 OVERVIEW

In Chapter 10 of *FSR* we introduce the two-variable regression model. As we discuss, this is another two-variable hypothesis test that amounts to fitting a line through a scatter plot of observations on a dependent variable and an independent variable. In this chapter, we walk you through how to estimate such a model in SPSS.

10.2 ESTIMATING A TWO-VARIABLE REGRESSION

The estimation of a two-variable regression model in SPSS, as discussed in Chapter 10 of *FSR*, is fairly straightforward. To practice, let's use the data set on opinions about government assistance to the poor under varying economic conditions (as measured by the unemployment rate) between 1975 and 2014. As always, the data are located in the directory "FSRSPSSFiles" on the computer that created this workbook. To navigate to that folder, we use the pull-down menus – "File" then "Open" then "Data" – and then change the drive and directory as necessary until we find the correct location where the data set is stored. The data file is called "GovtAsst.sav." Once you've found it, open it.[1]

In SPSS, we perform a regression analysis using the pull-down menu through clicking "Analyze," then "Regression," then "Linear. . . ." That will open a dialog box where we will choose which variables from the data set to analyze. A screenshot of that dialog box appears in Figure 10.1. The list of available variables to analyze is on the left part of the dialog box. Click on "Variable View" at the bottom of the screen to see their

---

[1] Again, all of the data sets we use can be found in the SPSS directory at www.cambridge.org/fsr.

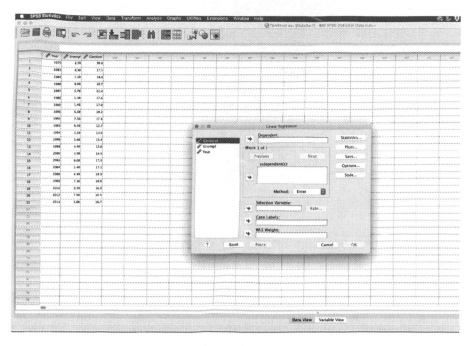

Figure 10.1 The linear regression dialog box in SPSS

descriptions. In order to perform the regression described in Section 10.3 of *FSR* – with percentage support for government assistance to the poor as the dependent variable, and unemployment rate as the independent variable – we select "GovAsst" from the list on the left, then click on the arrow to insert it in the "Dependent" box, and then click "Unempl" from the list on the left, and use the arrow to add it to the box of "Independent(s)." Then we click "OK."

A portion of the results from the output window appears in Figure 10.2. We say "a portion," because it's rather hard to deny that SPSS provides a heavy dose of information in its regression output. Near the bottom of the figure, in the portion labeled "Coefficients," you'll see the slope and Y-intercept that we estimated. Of greatest interest to us is the row labeled "Unempl," as this shows the relationship between the independent variable (unemployment rate) and our dependent variable (support for government assistance to the poor). In the column labeled "B," you'll see that the coefficient there is reported as 1.035. The row just above that, labeled "(Constant)," gives us the Y-intercept; in the column labeled "B," you'll see that the Y-intercept is 10.995. Altogether, that means that the formula for our regression line is $Y = 10.995 + 1.035X$, which (save for the number of digits provided) is exactly equal to the reported regression line in the text near the end of Section 10.3 in *FSR*.

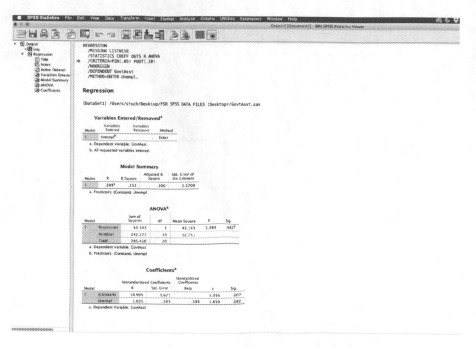

Figure 10.2 Bivariate regression output in SPSS

The next column over from the coefficients is labeled "Std. Error" – for "standard error" – as described in Section 10.4.4 of the main text. The t-test calculated in Section 10.4.5 in *FSR* can be replicated by looking at the output. When looking at the SPSS output, the coefficient (1.035) divided by its standard error (0.563) equals the calculated t-statistic (reported in the column "t" in the table) of 1.839. Note that this is the same as the calculated t in Section 10.4.6 of *FSR*. The last column of the SPSS output, labeled "Sig.," provides the exact p-value. In this case, the value reported there is 0.082. The best way to read that p-value is that it is "greater than 0.05," or, equivalently, that the relationship between unemployment rates and support for government assistance to the poor is not statistically significant at the 0.05 level.

SPSS provides other pieces of information that are of interest to us as well. The root mean-squared error described in Section 10.4.1 of the main text can be seen in Figure 10.2 here under the "Model Summary" portion near the top. It is in the column "Std. Error of the Estimate," which is another name for the root mean-squared error. The value there is 3.5709. That same portion of the output also shows the R-squared (or R^2) statistic, in the column labeled "R Square." The value there is 0.151.

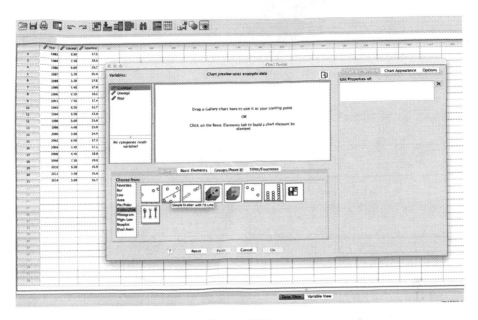

Figure 10.3 Graphing the regression line in SPSS

10.3 GRAPHING A TWO-VARIABLE REGRESSION

To better understand what is going on in a two-variable regression model, it is often helpful to graph the regression line. An example of this is presented in Figure 10.3 of *FSR*. We can produce a figure nearly identical to that by using SPSS's Chart Builder. Follow the procedures outlined in Chapter 9 of this workbook to produce a scatter plot, but instead of choosing the "Simple Scatter" from the "Gallery" menu, choose the "Simple Scatter with Fit Line" option. In Figure 10.3, the mouse is hovered above that option. Then choose the variables as you did in Chapter 9, and click "OK."

The results are displayed in Figure 10.4, which looks very similar to Figure 10.3 in *FSR*. By now, you're perhaps used to our small quibbles about the default chart title and axis labels. You can (and should!) double-click the chart to edit those to make more meaningful labels.

10.4 EXERCISES

1. Launch SPSS and open the "GovtAsst.sav" data set. Once you have done this, use the Chart Builder to produce, as closely as possible, Figure 10.3 from *FSR*. Copy and paste this figure into your word processing document.

2. If we change the independent variable in our running example from "unemployment" to "year," what would the theory of economic threat lead us to expect in terms of a hypothesis for the slope of a regression line with variabl

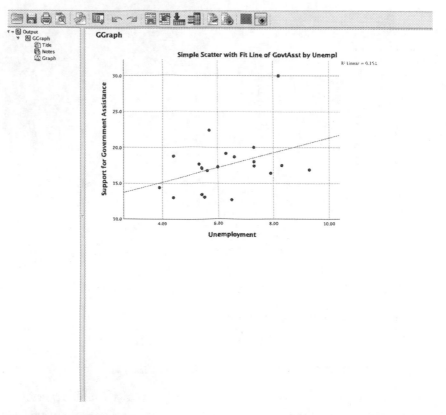

Figure 10.4 Output of a scatter plot with a regression line in SPSS

"inc_GovAsst" as the dependent variable and "year" as the independent variable? Explain your answer.

3. Estimate a regression model with the variable "inc_GovAsst" as the dependent variable and "year" as the independent variable.

(a) Copy and paste this output into your word processing document.

(b) Write about the results from the hypothesis test that you discussed above. What does this tell you about the theory of economic threat?

(c) Produce a figure like Figure 10.3 from *FSR* but with year as the independent variable (inc_GovAsst should remain as the dependent variable). Copy and paste this figure into your word processing document.

11 Multiple Regression

OVERVIEW

In Chapter 11 of *FSR*, we introduce the multiple regression model in which we are able to estimate the effect of X on Y holding Z constant. Here, we show you how to execute such models in SPSS.

ESTIMATING A MULTIPLE REGRESSION

The estimation of a multiple regression model, as discussed in Chapter 11 of *FSR*, is just an extension of the command used for estimating a two-variable regression. To practice, we'll use a slightly modified version of the data set that we used in Chapter 10. As always, the data are located in the directory "FSRSPSSFiles" on the computer that created this workbook. To navigate to that folder, we use the pull-down menus – "File" then "Open" then "Data" – and then change the drive and directory as necessary until we find the correct location where the data set is stored. The data file is called "GovtAsst_Chap11 .sav." Once you've found it, open it.[1]

In SPSS, we perform a multiple regression analysis using the pull-down menu through clicking "Analyze," then "Regression," then "Linear...." That will open the familiar dialog box from Chapter 10 of this workbook, where we will choose which variables from the data set to analyze. A screenshot of that dialog box appears in the previous chapter in Figure 10.1. The list of available variables to analyze are on the left part of the dialog box. Hover your mouse over those variables to see their descriptions. In order to estimate the multiple regression model displayed in column C in Table 11.3 of *FSR* – with percentage who support government assistance to the poor as the dependent variable, and with the

---

[1] Again, all of the data sets we use can be found in the SPSS directory at www.cambridge.org/fsr.

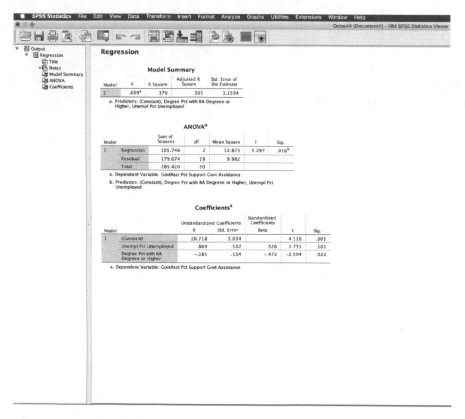

Figure 11.1 Multiple regression output in SPSS

unemployment rate and percentage with a B.A. degree or higher as the two independent variables – we select "GovtAsst" from the list on the left, then click on the arrow to insert it in the "Dependent" box, and then click "Unempl" from the list on the left, and use the arrow to add it to the box of "Independent(s)," and also click "Degree" from the list on the left and add that, also, to the box of "Independent(s)."[2] Then click "OK."[3]

Figure 11.1 shows a portion of the SPSS output. Compare the coefficients and their standard errors to those in column C in Table 11.3 of *FSR*. As before, there is the small difference between the number of digits past the decimal point presented. Otherwise, we trust that you find them to be identical. Interpreting the output is done in the same way as in Chapter 10 of this workbook and Chapter 11 of the main text.

[2] The order in which the independent variables appear does not matter; you will get the same results regardless of their order.

[3] In practice, you may have as many independent variables as you want in a regression model as long as you meet the minimum mathematical requirements that each independent variable varies, $n > k$, and you have no perfect multicollinearity. The first two of these requirements are discussed in Section 10.5.3 and the third is discussed in Section 11.8.1 of *FSR*.

11.3 FROM REGRESSION OUTPUT TO TABLE – MAKING ONLY ONE TYPE OF COMPARISON

As we discuss in Section 12.4 of *FSR*, when presenting the results from more than two regression models in the same table, it is important that we set up our comparisons appropriately – either as comparisons of different model specifications estimated with the same sample of data, or as the same model specification estimated with different samples of data. This is because if both the sample of data and the model specification change, then we cannot know for sure whether any differences in the estimates that we are observing are due to the different sample or the different specification.

11.3.1 Comparing Models with the Same Sample of Data, but Different Specifications

If your data set doesn't have any missing values for any of the variables that you want to include in a set of models with different specifications, then making a table for such comparisons is pretty straightforward. All that you need to do is estimate the regressions of interest to you, and then put them into separate columns of a table. But if, as is often the case, you have some missing values for some of the variables that you are including in your different models, then you need to take some extra steps in order to make sure that the regressions that you are comparing are all estimated with the exact same observations.

As an example of this, let's assume that the variable "Degree" is missing for the year 2010. Since regression models are based on only those cases that have no missing data on any of the variables in the model, it would be necessary for us to exclude the year for which the degree variable was missing.

Given that we know the year of the observation that we want to exclude, we can simply tell SPSS to select all cases where the value of the variable "year" is not equal to 2010. We do this by clicking on "Data," then "Select Cases…," which opens up a dialog box.

This is displayed in Figure 11.2. From this point, we choose the radio button "If condition is satisfied" and click the "If…" button, which opens yet another dialog box.

We now have to tell SPSS which criteria to use to select cases. You could, at this point, click on variable names and use the keypad in the dialog box, as displayed in Figure 11.3, but you can also just click in the white box at the top of that dialog box and type "year ne 2010" (where the "ne" means "is not equal to") and click "Continue," and then "OK." Then, if we went back and reran the bivariate regression of views toward government assistance and unemployment that we learned in Chapter 10,

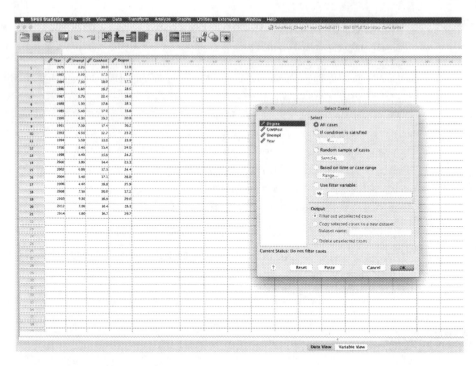

Figure 11.2 Selecting cases in SPSS

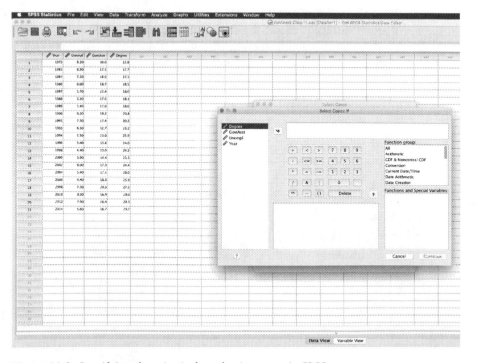

Figure 11.3 Specifying the criteria for selecting cases in SPSS

we would have the results (on twenty cases, instead of twenty-one) in column A of Table 11.3 of the main text.

It is important to remember one thing at this point: Unless you manually go back in the "Data" and "Select Cases..." menu to click on the "All cases" radio button at the top, SPSS will perform all subsequent analyses on the restricted sample of data. It's an easy thing to forget, so please be mindful of this feature.

It is worth reiterating that the procedure above only works when we know which variables are missing which observations. But what would we do if we didn't know exactly which observations are missing particular values of particular independent variables?[4] One of the easiest ways is just to estimate the model using all cases that are not missing for any of the independent variables that you plan to include in the models that you want to present. In our running example, we would need to click "Data," then "Select Cases...," then "If condition is satisfied," and the "If..." button, which opens yet again the familiar dialog box. Then we would type the following in the white command box at the top:

NOT(SYSMIS(unempl)|SYSMIS(degree))

and click "Continue" and "OK." From that point forward, our analyses would only be on nonmissing cases for "unempl" and "degree," which would create the output presented in the various columns of Table 11.3 in *FSR*.

And again, remember: Unless you manually go back in the "Data" and "Select Cases..." menu to click on the "All cases" radio button at the top, SPSS will perform all subsequent analyses on the restricted sample of data.

11.3.2 Comparing Models with the Same Specification, but Different Samples of Data

As an example of how to compare models with the same specification, but different samples of data, let's imagine that we want to look at the results from our running example of support for government assistance to the poor for observations after the turn of the twenty-first century compared with all observations before then. So, to estimate models on samples of data beginning in 2000 and all other cases, we would need to click "Data," then "Select Cases...," then "If condition is satisfied," and the "If..." button, which opens yet again the familiar dialog box. Then we would

---

[4] If an observation is missing for the dependent variable, it will not be included in any of the models that we estimate. Also, in general, we should have gotten to know our data before we estimate a regression model, and part of getting to know one's data is figuring out what are the missing values and why they are missing.

type "year => 2000" in the top box, click "Continue" and "OK," and run the regression model we want.

Then we would have to repeat the process, only this time substituting "year < 2000" into the top box, and rerun the regression model.

11.4 STANDARDIZED COEFFICIENTS

You may have noticed that SPSS automatically includes standardized coefficients in its multiple regression output. So if you look again at Figure 11.1, under the "Coefficients" section, you'll see a column labeled "Standardized Coefficients Beta." The values in that column are identical (save for the number of digits shown after the decimal points) to those computed in Section 11.6 of the main text.

11.5 DUMMY VARIABLES

As we discuss in Section 11.9 of *FSR*, dummy variables are categorical variables that take on one of two different values. The vast majority of the time in sociology, political science, and other social sciences, these two values are "zero" and "one." Dummy variables are usually created and named so that "one" represents the presence of a condition and "zero" represents the absence of that condition. In order to not confuse the people who will be reading your work or watching your presentations, it is a good idea to follow these conventions. For example, if you have a dummy variable to identify the gender identity of a survey respondent, it might be tempting to call the variable "gender." That, however, would leave unclear the issue of what the zeros and ones represent. If, by contrast, you named your variable "female," then the convention would be that a zero is for male respondents – or the absence of the condition "female" – and one is for the female respondents – the presence of the condition "female."

11.5.1 Creating a Dummy Variable in SPSS

Sometimes data sets that you are working with come with proper dummy variables already created for you. When they do not, you will need to create your own variables. There are multiple ways to create dummy variables in SPSS. In the "Transform" pull-down menu, there are two options that might seem like they serve the same function: "Recode into Same Variables..." and "Recode into Different Variables...." We strongly urge you to always use the "Recode into Different Variables..." option, as it greatly reduces the possibilities of you making a costly and irreversible

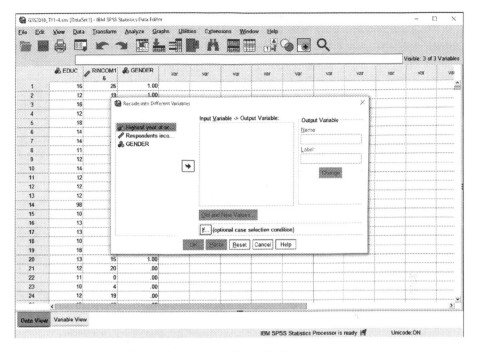

Figure 11.4 Creating a new dummy variable in SPSS

mistake. We will learn to do this using the data sets from the main *FSR* text, which include the 2016 General Social Survey.

As is our practice, the data are located in the directory "FSRSPSSFiles" on the computer that created this workbook. To navigate to that folder, we use the pull-down menus – "File" then "Open" then "Data" – and then change the drive and directory as necessary until we find the correct location where the data set is stored. The data file is called "GSS2016_T11-4 .sav." Once you've found it, open it.[5]

From the codebook for this study, we can tell that coding of values for each respondent's self-identified gender is in the variable named "Gender," and that the values of this variable are equal to 0 for "female" and 1 for "male." To check the values for this variable, let's look at a frequency distribution, as we learned in Chapter 7 of this workbook. Having seen that there are only values equal to 0 and 1 (and no others that we have to worry about or account for), we can now create the variable "female" and check what we have created using the "Recode into Different Variables…" command.

So click "Transform" on the pull-down menu, then "Recode into Different Variables…," which will open a dialog box like the one you

---

[5] A reminder: all of the data sets we use can be found in the SPSS directory at www .cambridge.org/fsr.

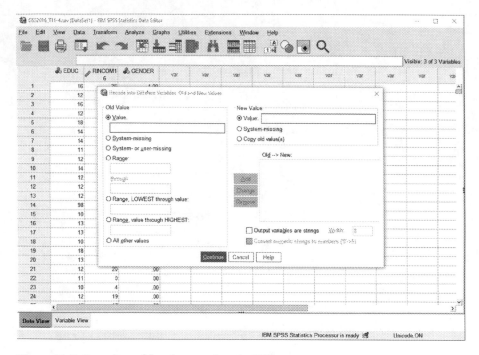

Figure 11.5 Recoding old and new values in SPSS

see in Figure 11.4. The first step is to pick the original variable, which is "Gender," from the list on the left-hand side, and use the blue arrow button to select it into the "Input Variable – > Output Variable" window. Next, on the far right-hand side of the dialog box, the "Output Variable" box will become active. We can type "female" in the "Name" box and "Gender of respondent" in the "Label" box. We then have to click the "Change" button just below those boxes.

Our next step is to click on the "Old and New Values" button, which opens up another embedded dialog box, as shown in Figure 11.5. Recall from above that, for the variable "Gender," males are coded 1, and in our new variable "female," we will have them recoded to 0. So in the "Old Value" portion of the new dialog box, we type 1 in the space marked "Value," and in the "New Value" portion, we type 0 in the space labeled "Value." Then, just below, click the "Add" button. Next, we need to recode the female respondents from 0 on "Gender" to 1, so type 0 in the "Old Value" window and 1 in the "New Value" window, and click "Add" again.[6] Then click "Continue" and "OK." Voilà. You've just created a new dummy variable.

---

[6] Obviously, you can see from Figure 11.5 that there are lots of other options for recoding variables, which may be of use to you in other circumstances.

Whenever you create a new variable, it is critically important to check that you created exactly what you intended to create. In this case, we could check our work with a tabular analysis, which (if we have done our work correctly) would show a perfect relationship between the old and new variables. So let's do that, and run a tabular analysis using the "Analyze," "Descriptive Statistics," and "Crosstabs…" selections from the pull-down menu. We would then need to put "Gender" and "female" into our rows and columns – it doesn't matter which one you put where – and click "OK." Doing so reveals that we have not misclassified any respondents.

11.5.2 Estimating a Multiple Regression Model with a Single Dummy Independent Variable

As we discussed in Section 11.2 of this workbook, the procedure for estimating a multiple regression with two (or more) independent variables is straightforward. We do this by using the pull-down menu through clicking "Analyze," then "Regression," then "Linear…." That will open the familiar dialog box from Chapter 10 of this workbook, where we will choose which variables from the data set to analyze. The list of available variables to analyze are on the left part of the dialog box. We select our dependent variable from the list on the left, then click on the arrow to insert it in the "Dependent" box, and then click whatever variables we want, one at a time, from the list on the left, and use the arrow to add them to the box of "Independent(s)."

As an example of this, we can estimate the regression model displayed on the right side of Table 11.4 of *FSR* from the 2016 GSS by using the variable "Rincom16" as the dependent variable (respondents' income), "Educ" as a continuous independent variable representing respondents' education (in years of schooling completed), and "Gender." Note that, as was the case with our multiple regression models with multiple continuous independent variables, the order of the independent variables does not matter for this command. The output from this command is displayed in Figure 11.6.

11.5.3 Estimating a Multiple Regression Model with Multiple Dummy Independent Variables

To estimate a multiple regression model with multiple dummy variables, you use the same procedure as in the previous section. The main complication comes when the multiple dummy variables represent values for a categorical variable with more than two values. As we discuss in Section 11.9.1 of *FSR*, in such a case, in order to avoid what is known

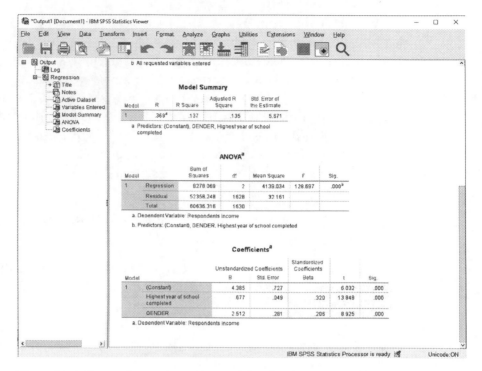

Figure 11.6 Output from a regression model with a dummy variable

as the "dummy variable trap," you need to leave one category of such an independent variable out of the regression model, and that left-out category becomes the "reference category."

11.6 DUMMY VARIABLES IN INTERACTIONS

In Section 11.10 of *FSR*, we discuss testing interactive hypotheses with dummy variables. There are several different ways to do this in SPSS. We recommend that you use a fairly straightforward approach where you start out by creating a new variable that is the multiplicative interaction between the dummy independent variable and the continuous independent variable. We'll again follow along the example from that section of the main text.

In order to create the interactive model displayed on the right side of Table 11.9 of *FSR*, we first create the interaction between the continuous variable "Educ" (the respondents' educational levels), and the dummy variable "Gender" with the following procedure. Under the "Transform" menu, click on "Compute Variable...." That will open a dialog box like the one shown in Figure 11.7. We need to give our new variable a name, so in the "Target Variable" box in the top left, type "educ_female" (though,

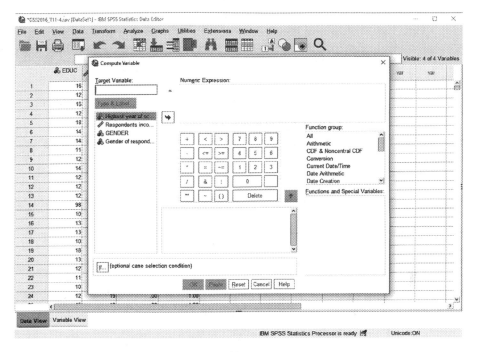

Figure 11.7 Creating an interaction variable

of course, you can name the variable anything). Beneath that box, click on the "Type & Label" box and type "Interaction of education and gender" and then click "Continue."

Back in the main dialog box for computing variables, we then define the interaction in the "Numeric Expression" box in the upper right. So, using the variable list along the left-hand side, click to find "Educ" and use the blue arrow to select it into the "Numeric Expression" box. Then type "*" (for multiplication), and then use the variable list again to click on "Gender" and use the blue arrow to move it into the "Numeric Expression" box. Your screen should look like the screenshot in Figure 11.8. Then click "OK."

So, to create the interactive model displayed on the right side of Table 11.9 of *FSR*, we simply run a linear regression model using the procedures we have already described, with the dependent variable being "Rincom16" (the respondents' incomes in 2016), and our three independent variables being "Educ" (the respondents' highest levels of educational attainment), the dummy variable "Gender," and our interaction variable "educ_female." When you run that model, you should get coefficients and standard errors like those in Figure 11.9, which (you will see) contains the same results as the "Interactive model" column in Table 11.9 of the main text.

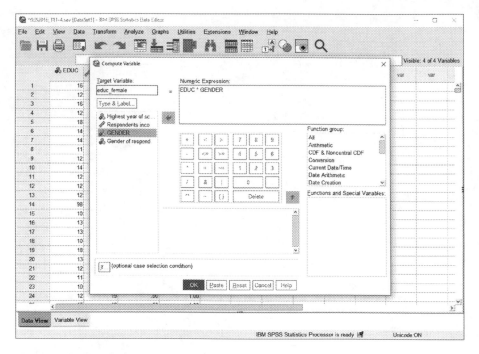

Figure 11.8 Details for creating an interaction variable

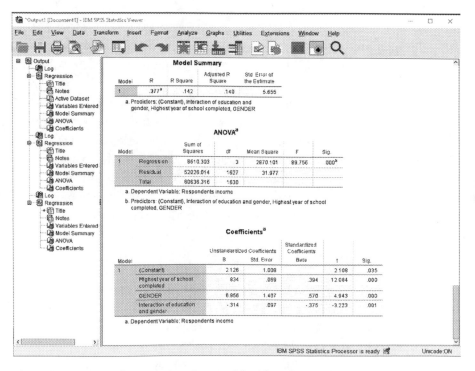

Figure 11.9 Output from a regression model with an interaction

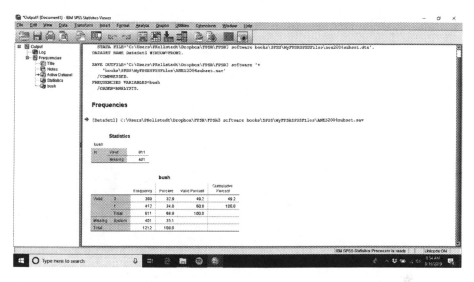

Figure 11.10 Frequency distribution for the variable "Bush"

11.7 MODELS WITH DUMMY DEPENDENT VARIABLES

As we discuss in Chapter 11 of *FSR*, there are several different models that can be used when we have a dummy dependent variable. We will learn to do this using the 2004 American National Election Study (ANES) – a survey of public opinion taken during that year's presidential campaign.

As is our practice, the data are located in the directory "FSRSPSSFiles" on the computer that created this workbook. To navigate to that folder, we use the pull-down menus – "File" then "Open" then "Data" – and then change the drive and directory as necessary until we find the correct location where the data set is stored. The data file is called "ANES2004subset.sav." Once you've found it, open it.[7]

In this set of examples, we will work with a dependent variable named "Bush," which equals 1 for respondents who reported that they voted for George W. Bush and equals 0 for those respondents who reported that they voted for John Kerry.[8] To get a look at the values for this variable, we can run a Frequencies command as we learned in Chapter 7 of this workbook.

Those values are displayed in Figure 11.10. As we discuss in Chapter 11 of *FSR*, one option when we have a limited dependent variable is simply to run a linear regression model using the procedures that we discussed earlier in this chapter of the workbook ("Analyze,"

---

[7] A reminder: all of the data sets we use can be found in the SPSS directory at www .cambridge.org/fsr.

[8] This is the same example that we use in Chapter 11 of *FSR*. For a more detailed explanation of the variable and how it was created, see footnote 19 at the beginning of Section 11.11.1 of *FSR*.

Figure 11.11 Calculating and displaying the predicted values from the linear probability model

"Regression," "Linear..."). So, if we want to estimate the model displayed in Table 11.10 of *FSR*, we would click the variable "bush" into the "Dependent" box, and click (in any order) the variables "partyid," "eval_WoT," and "eval_HoE" – where "partyid" is "Party Identification," "eval_WoT" is "Evaluation: War on Terror," and "eval_HoE" is "Evaluation: Health of the Economy" – into the "Independent(s)" box. We would next need to click on the "Save..." box, and check the box under "Predicted Values" for "Unstandardized." Then click "Continue," and "OK."

To calculate and summarize the predicted probabilities from this model, we would run descriptive statistics like we learned in Chapter 7 of this workbook ("Analyze," "Descriptive Statistics," "Frequencies...") on the predicted values we just generated from our regression. That variable should be called "PRE_1" – though SPSS gives these variables names automatically. Once you've selected the variable, click the "Statistics..." button and select the options as in Figure 11.4 of this workbook, and click "Continue" and then "OK."

This will produce the output displayed in Figure 11.11. If we look at the results – scrolling down in your output below what is in Figure 11.11 – we can see that we get some predicted values that are greater than 1. As we discuss in Chapter 11 of *FSR*, one of the problems of the linear probability model is that it can produce predicted probabilities that are greater than 1 or less than 0. This is one of the main reasons why sociologists, political scientists, and other social scientists prefer to use either a binomial logit

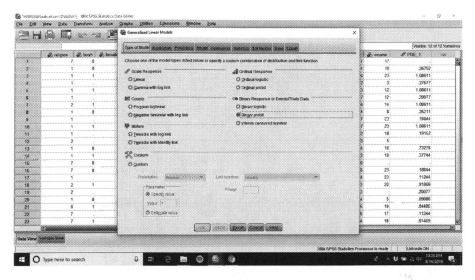

Figure 11.12 The Generalized Linear Models menu, with the "Binary probit" radio button selected

(BNL) model or a binomial probit (BNP) model when they have a dummy dependent variable.

To continue with our running example, we can produce the probit and logit columns of the results displayed in Table 11.11 of *FSR* – respectively, the "BNP" column and the "BNL" column – and predicted probabilities for each observation by running the following procedures.

To estimate a binomial probit model in SPSS, we use the pull-down menu and select "Analyze," then "Generalized Linear Models," and then again "Generalized Linear Models...," which opens a dialog box that is somewhat different than the linear regression dialog box.[9] That dialog box is shown in Figure 11.12. To run a binary probit model, we select the "Binary probit" radio button from the right-hand side of the "Type of Model" tab as displayed in the figure. To define our dependent variable, click on the "Response" tab at the top of the dialog box, and select your variable of interest and use the arrow key in the now-familiar way to click it into the "Dependent Variable" box.

By default, SPSS chooses the highest number as its reference category, but, by custom, most analysts choose the lowest value as the reference category. So click on the "Reference Category" button on the "Response" tab, and it will open another dialog box as displayed in Figure 11.13. Click on the "First (lowest value)" button and then click "Continue."

[9] You might think that a probit model would be estimated by clicking on "Analyze," "Regression," "Probit...," but that leads to a different procedure.

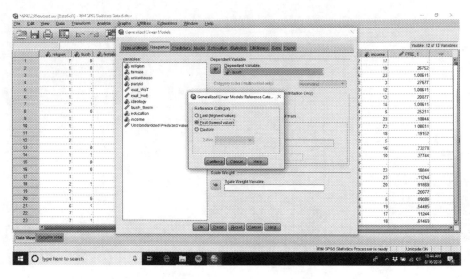

Figure 11.13 Changing the reference category in a binary probit model

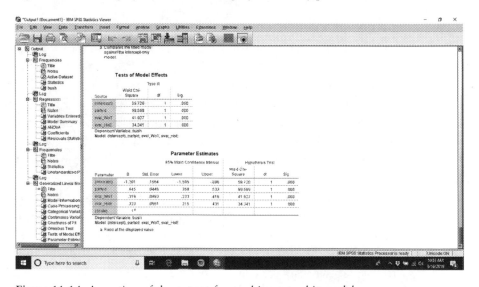

Figure 11.14 A portion of the output from a binary probit model

Next, click on the "Predictors" tab and, from the "Variables" list on the left, click your independent variables one by one (in any order) into the "Covariates" box. Next, click on the "Model" tab, and click all of your independent variables on the left (one at a time, in any order) and click the right arrow to move them all into the "Model" box on the right. Then click "OK" and you've run your model. The scrolled-down portion of the output is presented in Figure 11.14, and, as you'll see, those coefficients match the ones displayed in the "BNP" column in Table 11.11 of the main text.

To estimate a binomial logit model in SPSS, we have two options. We could follow the same procedure just described to estimate a binary probit model, except on the "Type of Model" tab displayed in Figure 11.12,

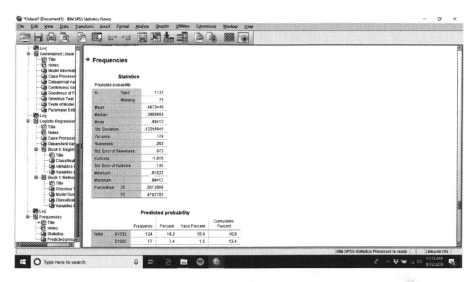

Figure 11.15 Displaying the predicted probabilities from the binary logit model

we would select "Binary logistic" instead of "Binary probit." The rest of the procedure is identical. Alternatively and equivalently, we could use the pull-down menu and select "Analyze," "Regression," "Binary Logistic...," which opens a dialog box that looks and functions much like the now-familiar linear regression dialog box, with its space for the dependent variable and the independent variables (called "Covariates" here). The benefit of the latter procedure is that it makes it easy to obtain predicted probabilities, as discussed in the main text, by clicking on the "Save..." button and clicking the box marked "Probabilities" under the "Predicted Values" section (and then clicking "Continue").

To summarize the predicted probabilities from this model, we would run descriptive statistics like we learned in Chapter 7 of this workbook ("Analyze," "Descriptive Statistics," "Frequencies...") on the predicted values we just generated from our binomial logit. As before, SPSS gives these variables names automatically, so you'll have to search for predicted probabilities in your list of variables. Once you've selected the variable, click the "Statistics..." button and select the options as in Figure 7.4 of this workbook, and click "Continue" and then "OK."

EXERCISES

1. Launch SPSS and open the "GovtAsst_Chap11.sav" data set. Once you have done this, run the commands to produce the output shown in Figure 11.1. Copy and paste this figure into your word processing document.

2. Estimate a multiple regression model with both Unemployment and Degree as the independent variables and GovtAsst as the dependent variable. Estimate

the two different two-variable models needed to produce the results in columns A and B of Table 11.3 of *FSR* where you are comparing the results across three specifications on the same sample of observations. Put your results into a table in your word processing document and write about what you have found.

3. Estimate the two multiple regression models described in this chapter with the same specification but where the sample is divided according to whether the observation occurred before or in or after 2000. Put these results into a table in your word processing document and write about what you have found.

4. Estimate a multiple regression model with standardized coefficients with Unemployment and Degree as the independent variables and views of Government support to the poor as the dependent variable. Put your results into a table in your word processing document and write about what you have found.

5. Launch SPSS and open the "GSS2016_T11-4.sav" data set. Once you have done this, run the procedure to produce the output shown in Figure 11.6. Copy and paste this into your word processing document.

6. Run the procedure to produce the output shown in Figure 11.9. Copy and paste this into your word processing document.

7. Create a dummy variable identifying female respondents. Estimate the model displayed in Figure 11.6 with this new variable instead of the variable identifying male respondents. Copy and paste this into your word processing document. Write a brief summary of what these results tell you.

8. Create an interaction between the new dummy variables that you created to identify female respondents and education. Estimate the model displayed in Figure 11.6 with this new variable instead of the variables identifying male respondents. Copy and paste this into your word processing document. Write a brief summary of what these results tell you.

9. Launch SPSS and open the "FairFPSR3.sav" data set. Once you have done this, run the procedure to produce the results presented in Table 11.11 of *FSR*. Copy and paste this figure into your word processing document.

10. Calculate the proportionate reduction in error from a naive model to the BNL and from a naive model to the BNP. Write briefly about what you have learned from doing this.

12 Putting It All Together to Produce Effective Research

12.1 OVERVIEW

In Chapter 12 of *FSR*, we tie the broad lessons of the book together in order to help you on your way to producing compelling research. In the last chapter of this companion book, we have some exercises for you to get you moving in this direction.

12.2 EXERCISES

1. Launch SPSS and open the "GSS2016_Sample_Chap12.sav" data set. Once you have done this, you'll see that there are five variables in this subsample from the 2016 GSS, as pictured in Figure 12.1: year (2016 only), educ (highest year of schooling completed), sex (male or female), rincom16 (respondent's income in 2016), and race (non-Hispanic whites and non-Hispanics blacks only). Rincom16 will be the dependent variable in the exercises for this chapter. Run the commands necessary to output appropriate descriptive statistics for the dependent variable (including a box–whisker plot) and write a brief summary of what you have found. Copy and paste the box–whisker plot into your word processing document.

2. Estimate a two variable regression model with rincom16 as the dependent variable and education as the independent variable. Write about what you have found. Copy and paste the output into your word processing document.

3. Estimate a multiple regression model with educ, sex (coded 1 for females and 0 for males), and race (coded 1 for non-Hispanic blacks and 0 for non-Hispanic whites) as independent variables, and rincom16 as the dependent variable. Put your results into a table in your word processing document and write about what you have found.

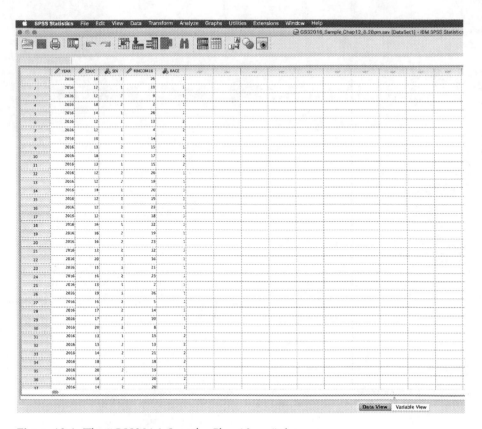

Figure 12.1 The "GSS2016_Sample_Chap12.sav" data set

4. Estimate the same multiple regression model as above but reverse the coding of both dummy variables so that males are coded 1 and females are coded 0, and non-Hispanic whites are coded 1 and non-Hispanic blacks are coded 0. Put these results into a table in your word processing document and write about what you have found.

5. Estimate a multiple regression model with standardized coefficients with education and the dummy variables for sex and race as the independent variables, and rincom16 as the dependent variable. Put your results into a table in your word processing document and write about what you have found.

6. Create an interaction term between the dummy variables that you created for female and non-Hispanic black respondents. Then estimate a multiple regression model with education, the dummy variables for females and non-Hispanic blacks, and the interaction term as the independent variables, and rincom16 as the dependent variable. Compare your results with those in Figure 12.2. Copy and paste this into your word processing document. Write a brief summary of what these results tell you.

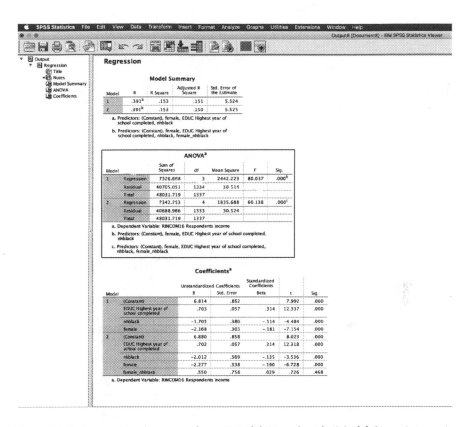

Figure 12.2 Regression output without (Model 1) and with (Model 2) an interaction term

References

Bansak, Kirk, Jens Hainmueller, and Dominik Hangartner. 2016. "How Economic, Humanitarian, and Religious Concerns Shape European Attitudes Toward Asylum Seekers." *Science* 354(6309):217–222.

Branton, Regina P., and Bradford S. Jones. 2005. "Reexamining Racial Attitudes: The Conditional Relationship Between Diversity and Socioeconomic Environment." *American Journal of Political Science* 49(2):359–372.

Esses, Victoria M., John F. Dovidio, Lynne M. Jackson, and Tamara L. Armstrong. 2001. "The Immigration Dilemma: The Role of Perceived Group Competition, Ethnic Prejudice, and National Identity." *Journal of Social Issues* 57(3):389–412.

King, Gary, Benjamin Schneer, and Ariel White. 2017. "How the News Media Activate Public Expression and Influence National Agendas." *Science* 358(6364): 776–780.

McLaren, Lauren M. 2003. "Anti-immigrant Prejudice in Europe: Contact, Threat Perception, and Preferences for the Exclusion of Migrants." *Social Forces* 81(3):909–936.

Perry, Samuel L., Ryon J. Cobb, Andrew L. Whitehead, and Joshua B. Grubbs. 2021. "Divided by Faith (in Christian America): Christian Nationalism, Race, and Divergent Perceptions of Racial Injustice." *Social Forces*, soab134, https://doi.org/10.1093/sf/soab134.

Scarborough, William J., Joanna R. Pepin, Danny L. Lambouths III, Ronald Kwon, and Ronaldo Monasterio. 2021. "The Intersection of Racial and Gender Attitudes, 1977 through 2018." *American Sociological Review* 86(5):823–855.

Sullivan, Jas M., and Alexandra Ghara. 2015. "Racial Identity and Intergroup Attitudes: A Multiracial Youth Analysis." *Social Science Quarterly* 96(1):261–272.

Index

Printed in the United States
by Baker & Taylor Publisher Services